Learning chess

Manual for
chess trainers

Step 4

Rob Brunia, Cor van Wijgerden

2nd edition 2013

ISBN 978-90-77275-49-8

Information: www.stappenmethode.nl

E-mail: info@stappenmethode.nl

Publisher: Cor van Wijgerden
English translation: Bert Botma, Ian Adams
Proofreading: Ian Adams
Drawings: Rupert van der Linden
Cover design: Eric van der Schilden

Contents

Preface

The Step-by-Step method has been officially acknowledged by the Dutch Chess Federation. It has been successfully adopted by many chess clubs and schools in the Netherlands, Belgium, France, Germany, Switzerland and Austria. Slowly but steadily the method is gaining popularity throughout the world. Step 1 is already available in 7 languages.

The course consists of manuals, aimed specifically at chess teachers and trainers, basic workbooks, extra workbooks and plus workbooks for students.
The course introduces the game of chess in a no-nonsense, common-sense way to players from ages 6 up. It introduces many psychological aspects of the game and avoids the pitfalls that characterise many less extensive courses. It allows anyone of average and above average ability to absorb – at his or her own pace – the chess rules and skills which are required in order to become a strong club player. It also tries to remove most of the impediments which cause players to play below their strength.

The difficulty level of the material in the fourth Step is higher than in Step three. That is why a good command of and the ability to apply the topics from the third Step are absolutely necessary.
Two new workbooks have been added to the course: Step 4 extra and Step 4 plus.

At present all the books but one of the chess course have been translated into English. Updated information can be found at our website, at:
www.stappenmethode.nl

For more information, please contact info@stappenmethode.nl

Enjoy your chess lessons!

Coevorden, October 2013
Cor van Wijgerden

The fourth Step

It is advisable to follow the lessons in Step 4 only if the previous Steps have been successfully completed. This means not only that the students have passed the relevant exams, but also that they have managed to apply the relevant knowledge to their own games. If the students lack the skills required for Step 4, presenting them with new information is likely to be counterproductive.

As regards the trainer, we assume that he or she is familiar with the didactic approach as outlined in the previous manuals.

Subject material

The level of difficulty of the material in Step 4 is significantly higher than that in the third Step. This is mainly due to the increase in the amount of moves required to solve the assignments. For most exercises the solution is 2½ moves deep (i.e. 5 ply).

As they do, tactics will continue to play an important role in the students' games. In this Step we focus on the last two forms of eliminating the defender, i.e. interfering and blocking. Students will like the second form in particular.

In Step 4, double attacks will be seen to require a preparatory move, since otherwise a double attack is ineffective. We will consider all types of preparatory moves: luring, eliminating the defender, chasing, aiming and clearing.

We will introduce the concept of the preparatory move in the lesson that deals with the placement of the front and the back piece. Other aspects of the pin will not be discussed until Step 5.

Other tactical topics that will be covered include the 7th rank and the magnet. In addition, we will start to focus on some positional aspects, since at Step 4 level these begin to play a (modest) role in the students' games. Endgames are especially suitable for introducing positional aspects, given that positional play is less concrete than tactical play. The lesson on material advantage and endgame strategy focuses on a number of strategic issues. The lesson on weak pawns will make the students a bit more aware of how to play with pawns. The same goes for the lesson on the opening. In general, it is a good idea to discuss positional factors in relation to the students' own games (see also the concept of 'mini plan' as introduced in Step 3).

Attacks on the king involve a mixture of tactics and strategy. In this Step we focus first and foremost on how to finish off such attacks.

In chess it is important to plan one's actions. Planning plays an important role in the 'Queen versus pawn' lesson. This lesson further underscores the importance of piece cooperation and the relative nature of the value of pieces.

It goes without saying that the specific choice of the topics addressed is a matter of personal taste, based on one's knowledge of and one's experience with the way in which children develop their chess skills.

Chess games

This subject has been dealt with extensively in previous Steps, especially in the manual of Step 3 (under 'Training games'). Unfortunately, much of the training that children receive at clubs is limited to instruction and exercises.

It is essential that the children play positions against each other. This serves a number of purposes:

1) Practising practical skills in specific positions.
2) Getting acquainted with a particular theme of the opening, middlegame or endgame.
3) Creating more varied training sessions (by introducing a competitive element).

It is important that the positions offer a clear illustration of the topic under discussion, so as to guarantee that the children develop specific skills (see 1 above). In this respect the playing strength of the trainer is clearly relevant. When the children are getting acquainted with a new theme (see 2 above) the trainer can check the knowledge that is already present, and so provide new information that suits the specific needs of the children. As regards under 3, it is important that the training sessions involve a good balance of theory and practice. Periods during which the children should be quiet and pay attention should be complemented with periods during which the children can play chess. This setup will allow the children to absorb the theory once more during practical play.

The way in which a position is played to a finish is also important. The position should not be so one-sided as to bore the children and make them lose their motivation. To prevent this, the children should play each position twice, once with Black and once with White. When playing, it is a good idea to ask the students to note down their moves. In this way the games can be discussed on the demonstration board afterwards. With this format none of the children will feel left out. Note, too, that each of the game positions must illustrate a certain point: the children must not have the feeling that the exercise in question did not serve any purpose. On a final note, it often happens that a game has to be stopped or interrupted through lack of time. It is important to realise that young players like to finish their games. The trainer runs the risk of being seen as a spoil-sport. Children of all ages like to win, no matter what the goal of the exercise is.

Thinking ahead

The skill of thinking ahead is practised independently through discussions of a position (see also lesson 5). The individual skills of both trainers and students are different and this aspect of the training varies with it. The ease with which a trainer can handle a position will inspire the students. For this reason, the trainer must have reasonably good chess skills.

If the trainer's skills are insufficient, then this can be partly compensated for by means of intensive preparation. The varying speed of development of the students calls for separate measures. Discipline during training and the opportunity to do individual work both contribute to a successful training session. This means that when doing the exercises:

- everyone should remain silent.
- the moves have to be performed slowly.
- if someone suggests a different move, then the whole variation has to be repeated.
- the trainer decides whose turn it is.

If these principles are maintained from the beginning it will provide structure to the training. As regards individual differences between students, there are several possibilities:

- when thinking ahead for a number of moves, the weaker students may execute the first move(s) on their board.
- adjusting the way in which the questions are asked, so that a weaker student has to give one possible move only, while a stronger student has to look for the best move.
- setting up a position at the end of the variation allows the trainer to differentiate between students.
- dividing the group into smaller groups, based on the number of moves that students should think ahead.
- answering different questions about the position in which thinking ahead is required.

This list is, of course, not exhaustive. The best method will depend on the group, the situation and the trainer's inventiveness.

When setting up a 'thinking ahead' position, it is advisable to adhere to the following rules:

- the starting position must not be visible on any other board (e.g. the demonstration board or a neighbour's board).
- a piece put on the board, may not be moved.
- there is a limited thinking time (approximately 30 seconds to a minute).

- everyone starts on an empty board.

This will allow the trainer to verify whether the final position is correct.

Help

The help that is offered to the students in Step 4 strongly resembles that of the previous Step. Here, too, the trainer asks the student to formulate the problem and point out the error (See Manual Step 3 for further information).

Each lesson has a 'Help' section (which can be found in the Workbook section) that contains some additional pointers, including some hints for the occasional more difficult exercise. The forms of help outlined above are not repeated in each of the lessons.

The material in Step 4 relates to the material covered in previous Steps. As such, the trainer should be able to recognise the nature of the mistakes made by the students. If the nature of a mistake suggests that a student has insufficiently mastered an earlier topic, then this earlier topic should be revised. This is important, because it is pointless to introduce a new topic if an earlier topic has not been sufficiently mastered.

Apart from spotting the correct type of combination, the students must also learn to find the right preparatory move. The trainer must then be able to see whether the mistake lies in the type of combination or in the type of preparatory move.

During Step 4, individual differences will arise in the students' internalisation of knowledge and skills. Some students require assistance in order to keep making progress. This assistance must be regarded first and foremost as individual support. The mistakes made by the students may indicate that a change is required in the setup of the lessons, the instruction, or the speed with which new material is presented. More generally, these mistakes demonstrate that old material should be repeated from time to time.

For the trainer, both the nature of the students' mistakes and their problems are a source of feedback. He can use this feedback to develop a tailor-made approach for the group in question. Note that a high number of questions reflects uncertainty on the part of a group. This warrants a reaction on the part of the trainer:
- The speed with which new material is introduced must be reduced.
- The material that is presented is too difficult.

Adapting the speed and/or the degree of difficulty gives the students back their confidence. It will also help the students to tackle the relatively more difficult topics. The more the students progress, the more indirect the trainer's assistance becomes. And the more they progress, the more ambitious they become and the more willing they are to tackle new topics.

Given this, the trainer should bear in mind that introducing new material at an increased speed is likely to give the students superficial knowledge only. This may in turn lead to a loss of acquired knowledge and stagnation in the students' development. If this problem is recognised, and these pitfalls are avoided, then this will lead to a lasting and successful increase of the students' playing strength.

Applying the knowledge

The children have acquired a lot of knowledge in the first four Steps. By looking at the children's games the trainer can see whether this knowledge is being applied to their games. It is only natural that there is a difference between the children's level of knowledge and level of skill (i.e. playing level). The trick is to keep this gap as small as possible. Failure to watch out for this will result in a loss of motivation on the part of the students, because they will then not see their efforts rewarded in terms of an increase in playing strength. Being the best during the lessons does not make up for losing every single game. Chess training includes both training and playing. The trainer should therefore strive for a balanced approach.

By discussing a game we establish a link between the chess training and the students' games. The student begins by explaining what he thought of his game. Then the trainer points out some of the aspects to which extra attention must be paid. For the student this means that he must learn to apply, or to better apply, material that he has already mastered. For instance, the trainer might point out that in his game the student missed a double attack with the queen.

Discussing students' games is especially useful when it comes to positional aspects. Such aspects are easier to consider in relation to a game than in a lesson. In addition to the students' games from competitions, the trainer can also use games from a simultaneous training format or games that the students have played against each other during a training session. No matter which games or game positions are used, feedback is always useful.

It is a pity that in the majority of youth tournaments the amount of thinking time is limited. Even regional youth championships are often decided by rapid games. This means that students do not usually note down their moves, and thus that no feedback can be given. A player who evaluates a position thoroughly could easily exceed the time limit. As a result, there is the risk of an inverse relation between knowledge and result. Students benefit from playing tournament games with ample thinking time.

The transition to the seniors

Not many children will reach Step 4 level. Many of them drop out because there are not enough sufficiently strong trainers or because they have gone through the previous Steps too quickly. The students' motivation will quickly vanish when they notice that their playing strength is not increasing.

The drawback of training small groups makes it impossible to organise a good competition. It is boring to have to play the same opponent time and time again. In many clubs this is solved by letting the students play with the seniors. The problem of moving children to the senior division is essentially the same as that of allowing children to go to bed late, or to force them to adapt socially to their seniors (consider 11-13 year-olds). The children's chess development will stagnate because they will subconsciously adapt their playing style to that of adults. Their sharp attacking games make way for careful play, so they will not lose too quickly. Our aim is to increase the chess skills of young people and so we should be more careful when it comes to the transition from junior to senior player. Acquiring practical skills should not be restricted to the few chosen ones who are allowed to appear at tournaments. The idea that young players should play with senior players might hold water when they are 15 or older. However, for 12-year-old (or even younger) players this is not a good idea. In this case another setup must be found. In the past many young players have dropped out because of stagnation. This loss is, of course, unnecessary.

For youth clubs in the same region, one possibility would be to organise a joint competition for the higher Steps. This makes it possible for young people of the same playing strength to play against each other. The risk that a young player will go on to join a 'competing' club should then just be accepted. At least he will continue to play chess.

Analysing a position

As to the quality of a move in a particular position, a number of factors are relevant
1) the students' knowledge
2) the students' skill of evaluating different possibilities
3) the students' skill of visualising and thinking ahead
Points 1 and 3 will receive direct attention in this manual. Point 2 also requires attention, given that it is possible to teach students a systematic approach for analysing positions. Evaluating the possible moves in a particular position involves a number of different skills:

- eliminating
- comparing
- the depth of the search
- (daring) to draw a conclusion

Visualising and thinking ahead will be hardly necessary when the students are allowed to examine the position with their hands on the pieces. Eliminating involves leaving obvious incorrect moves out of further consideration. Comparing involves weighing one possibility against another. This will create many problems, since it is not clear how deep the students should look and which conclusions they should draw. Here the students' level of knowledge becomes relevant. Armed with more knowledge, students can make a more insightful decision. There are two reasons why students fail to come up with a move in due time: either the search depth is too great or they are afraid to draw a conclusion.

Certificate

After having gone through the lessons of Step 4, the students can take an exam. When they pass this exam they will receive a certificate. The certificate is not a goal in itself. The aim of the chess lessons is first and foremost to build and raise the students' chess skills ('how to learn and play better chess'), not to obtain certificates. However, certificates can be a good stimulus to continue with the course right to the end.

We must also realise that giving children the prospect of a certificate at the beginning of the year will not stimulate them for very long. The point at which they will receive the certificate lies too far ahead in the future. Short-term goals serve as a better stimulus.

When preparing for the exam it is sensible to let the students do a test exam first and, if necessary, a second time. However, it is not advisable to have the students do too many test exams, as this will put a severe strain on their enthusiasm and place too much emphasis on the exams and certificates.

How to use this manual

The manual contains many split diagrams. These must be read and set up on the board as separate diagrams. The left part of a diagram must therefore be set up on an empty demonstration board (i.e. without the position on the right). When discussing the right part, the position on the left has to be removed. Leaving that position on the board is not a good idea, since this often leads to misunderstandings.

The following symbols, which refer to diagrams, are of crucial importance:
⇧ refers to the diagram on the top of the page.
⇨ refers to the diagram in the middle of the page.
⇩ refers to the diagram at the bottom of the page.

The moves in the answers are sometimes accompanied by an exclamation mark or a question mark, e.g.. **1. Qxc7!** or **1. ... Re2?**
The exclamation mark represents a good move.
The question mark represents a bad move.

The name of the reminder – if present – and the exercise sheets of the relevant lesson can be found in the exercises under the heading **Workbook**. The diamond is the name of the reminder, the square is the name of the exercise sheet. They can be found in the workbook.
◊   *Draws*
□   *Endgame / Passed pawn: A*   ♖

The degree of difficulty is indicated by means of the number of rooks. The sheets marked '♖' can be done by everyone after the lesson. The sheets marked '♖ ♖' are more difficult and are intended only for the occasional student. They are strongly advised for everyone, but only at a later phase in the training. Most children will not get to the sheets marked '♖ ♖ ♖'. These exercises are useful only at the end of the Step or during a subsequent Step, in which case they are ideal test exercises.

1   Opening advantage

AIM OF THE LESSON
- using the opening as a weapon

PRIOR KNOWLEDGE
- the 3 golden rules (see 2nd step)
- completing the opening (see 3rd step)

ACQUISITION

Instruction
A good start is to ask the students what they know about the opening.

A lead in development
This lesson deals with the advantage of having a lead in development. To illustrate this, one side will follow the 3 golden rules to the letter while the other side does not.

The position of the diagram (⇨) arises after **1. e4 e5 2. Nf3 Nc6 3. Bc4 h6 4. Nc3 a6**. While White has brought out three pieces, Black has brought out only one.
White, then, is ahead in development. The white pieces are active. They control the centre and exert an influence on squares on the opponent's side of the board. In order to exploit this advantage, White's other pieces will have to find targets to attack. These pieces must be given sufficient space to manoeuvre and thus should be activated.
One solution would be to open up the position with **5. d4**, since after **5. ... exd4 6. Nxd4 Nxd4 7. Qxd4** (diagram ⇩) White's pieces occupy good positions.
White only needs a further two moves to

complete his development, whereas Black needs no fewer than five. Furthermore, White has an iron grip on the centre, especially on the d5-square, which he controls 4 times. As a result, Black has nothing better than the modest developing move d6.

A possible continuation is **7. ... d6 8. Be3 Nf6 9. 0-0-0 Be7** (diagram ⇧).

Now that White has finished his development, it is time to increase the activity of his pieces. White has two attractive possibilities.

Plan 1: open the position with 10. e5.

This move presents Black with a problem on account of the weak position of his king. Moving away loses a pawn immediately: 10. ... Ng4 11. exd6 Bf6 12. Qe4+.

Chasing the queen away also does not help: 10. ... c5 11. Qf4 g5 12. Qg3 and the pawn on d6 is lost.

This leaves **10. ... dxe5 11. Qxe5 Bd7** (diagram ⇨), after which White has two attractive choices: **12. Rhe1 0-0 13. Bxh6** is strong, as is **12. Nd5 Rc8** (12. ... Nxd5 13. Qxd5 Be6 14. Qxb7) **13. Nxf6+ gxf6 14. Qh5 Th7 15. Rhe1**.

Plan 2: playing for an attack on the king.

From the diagram (⇧) White can continue with **10. f3 0-0 11. g4**, opening lines on the kingside. This is a promising plan, since Black has played the weakening ... h7-h6, which gives White a target for his attack and allows him to open lines. Show the students that White would be unable to open lines if the black pawn were on h7. Now Black must be careful. He is in danger after **11. ... Be6 12. h4 Qd7 13. g5** while after **13. ... hxg5 14. hxg5 Nh7 15. e5 dxe5 16. Qh4** (diagram ⇩) he is lost.

White's lead in development has enabled him to:
• take control of the centre

14

- convert a temporal advantage into an attack on the king
- open lines
- organise a kingside attack

Opening the position
An important principle in opening play is that if you have an opening advantage, then you must open up the game. One way in which this can be done is by exchanging pawns in the centre, thus clearing diagonals and files.
Sometimes it is also possible to open up a position by means of a sacrifice. An example:
1. e4 e5 2. Nf3 Nc6 3. Nc3 g6 4. d4
Opening the diagonal of the c1-bishop and attacking e5.
4. ... exd4 5. Nd5
This is not a move that a grandmaster would play, but suitable for Step 4 level.
5. ... Bg7 6. Bg5 (see diagram ⇨)
Time to take stock. Ask the students to find a move for Black, using their own boards.

6. ... Nf6 runs into 7. e5, winning a piece. White also nets a piece after 6. ... Bf6 7. Nxf6+ Nxf6 8. e5. While 6. ... f6 cannot be directly refuted, this move hampers Black's development. After 7. Bh4 White exercises strong pressure on f6. With the a2-g8 diagonal available for the f1-bishop, Black will find it hard to castle.
6. ... Nge7.
7. Nf6+ is not bad as after it Black loses either the right to castle or the control of the black squares (after 7. ... Bxf6 8. Bxf6). However, even better is the powerful:
7. Nxd4
which wins a piece. The threat is 8. Nxc6 (eliminating the defender). 7. ... Nxd4 is met by 8. Bxe7. The way White finishes off the game is pretty.
7 ... Bxd4 (see diagram ⇩) **8. Qxd4 Nxd4 9. Nf6+ Kf8 10. Bh6#**.

Openings in which a pawn is sacrificed are called gambits (from the Italian word *gambetta* 'lift a leg'). The purpose of a gambit is to gain time in the opening.

To conclude this chapter we discuss one example of a gambit, the King's Gambit. In the line that we consider, Black brings out his queen too early and plays too many pawn moves.
1. e4 e5 2. f4 exf4 3. Nf3 d6 4. Bc4 Be6 5. Bxe6 fxe6 6. d4 (diagram ⇧) **6. ... Qf6.**
Black wants to maintain his pawn on f4, but here his queen obstructs the g8-knight and is vulnerable. White's advance of the e5-pawn will now be with a gain of tempo.
7. Nc3 Ne7 8. Qe2 c6 (see diagram ⇨)
It is better to develop the b8-knight.
9. e5 dxe5
This move loses instantly. It is preferable to play 9. ... Qh6, though White is very comfortable after 10. Ne4.
10. Ne4
Black might as well give up the game. The queen has nowhere to go to (10. ... Qg6 11. Nxe5 or 10. ... Qh6 11. Nd6+ and 12. Nf7).

It is a good idea to start introducing the topics of this lesson (i.e. increasing one's activity, gain of tempo, increasing your opponent's vulnerability) to the discussion of the student's games.

Search strategy
The sheets that accompany this lesson are mixed sheets with exercises from previous Steps. These exercises will continue to present problems if the correct search strategy is not followed:
• first consider the characteristics of the position
• then search for possible moves
• finally, check the move(s) found

The ideal practice for this lesson is a simultaneous display, in which extra attention is paid to this lesson's subject matter.
Students who have finished their game could go on to do an exercise page. Go over the correct search strategy using a position from an exercise sheet.

Workbook

☐ *Test / Mix (2nd + 3rd step): A*

Explanation: The themes of the assignments are given together with the answers. Ask the students to indicate some of the themes involved. This will help them to find the answers.

Mistake: The correct answer is not found.

Help: When a student fails to see the answer through recognition of the type of position, the search strategy should be used. Ask the student to first indicate the characteristics of the position (targets!) and then ask for a solution strategy. This will help most students to find the answer. If this fails, then more direct questions are in order. These will depend on the theme of the exercise.

☐ *Test / Mix (2nd + 3rd step): B*

Explanation: See exercise page A.

Mistake: Position 4 is not correctly solved.

Help: What is the bishop on c3 doing? It is attacking g7 and it is also pinning the pawn, so that h6 is not protected. How can White attack this pawn? The answer is clear: by chasing away the rook from the f4 square.

Mistake: Position 9 is not correctly solved.

Help: This position is difficult because the attention of the students will be concentrated on the attack on d5. One option is to alter the position by adding a white pawn on e4. 1. Rc6+ is then easy to see. We take away the pawn again, point out (but do not play!) 1. Rc6+, and ask what happens if Black captures the rook on d5. If this does not help, then execute the rook move and, if necessary, also Black's reply. This will reduce the problem to a Step 1 exercise.

ANSWERS

☐ *Test / Mix (2nd + 3rd step): A*

1) 1. Qb4 threatens mate and material gain (double attack: queen)
2) 1. ... Qd2+ 2. Qxd2 Rg6# (luring away + mate); 1. ... Rg6+? 2. Qxg6 hxg6 3. Kxg6+ and wins.
3) 1. Ng6 (trapping thanks to pinning)
4) 1. ... Re1+ 2. Rxe1 Qxd4+ (luring away + material); 2. Kf2 Re2+
5) 1. Bxf6 Qxf6 2. Qh7# (capturing + mate)
6) 1. Rh5+ gxh5 2. Qf6# (luring away+ mate)
7) 1. ... Bg6 (pin)
8) 1. Rf3+ exf3 2. Qxg5 (discovered attack)
9) 1. Nc6+ Ka8 2. Nxe7; 1. ... Rxc6 2. dxc6 (double attack: knight)
10) 1. b4 (trapping)
11) 1. ... Ra6+ 2. Kxa6 (forcing stalemate)
12) 1. 0-0-0+ and 2. Nxb5 (defending against a pin)

☐ *Test / Mix (2nd + 3rd step): B*

1) 1. Qxh7+ Rxh7 2. Ng6# (capturing + mate)
2) Drawing
3) 1. Nd6+ Qxd6 2. Ba6# (discovered attack)
4) 1. g3 Rxf3 2. Qxh6+ Qh7 2. Bxg7+ (attack on a pinned piece)
5) 1. ... Nf3+ 2. Qxf3 Qe1+ (discovered attack)
6) 1. Bd6 Bxd6 2. Qh8# (discovered attack)
7) 1. ... Ba4 (trapping thanks to a pin)
8) 1. ... Nxf3+ 2. Nxf3 R8g2# (capturing + mate)
9) 1. Rc6+ Kf7 (1. ... Kxd5 2. Bg2#) 2. Rxe5 (chasing away + material)
10) 1. Ne5+ Ke8 2. Rxc8# (double check)
11) 1. ... Rb8 (trapping)
12) 1. ... Rc3+ 2. Kxc3 (forcing stalemate); 2. Kb2? Kxb4

18

* learning a new attacking technique

* eliminating the defender (capturing, chasing away, luring away)

Instruction

In addition to capturing, chasing away and luring away, interfering is the 4th way of eliminating the defender. It is the most surprising of the four, since, another piece besides the attacker and the defender, is involved: the interfering piece.

Interfering + material
In the diagram (⇨) the bishop is protected by the rook on h5. The rook cannot be captured, and chasing it away is pointless: **1. ... g6** is met by **2. Rd5** or **2. Rh7+**. With **1. ... g5+** the pawn, with tempo, interferes with the protection which the rook is offering to the bishop. The b5-bishop is no longer protected and after White has got out of check, Black is free to take it.

In the left of the diagram (⇩) White's queen is attacking the b1-rook, which is protected by the queen on b7. White can interfere with that with **1. Bb6+**, eliminating the queen's protection of the rook. Black's best chance is to give up the exchange with **1. ... Rxb6**.
On the right part White plays **1. g5**, after which the rook on h4 is lost. The queen must give up the protection of the rook.
These examples are of the type: interfering + material. The interfering piece can always be

captured (of course!), but the attacker is in no danger of losing material. The piece is safe. Things will be different in the following examples, most of the time the interfering move will be a sacrifice.

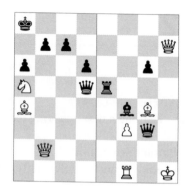

Interfering + mate
The diagram (⇧) contains a position in which the goal is mate, and the means is interfering. White cannot give mate as long as Black's queen is protecting b7. With **1. Bc6** White closes off the queen's diagonal; **1. ... bxc6** is followed by **2. Qb7** mate. It is important that the bishop is also eyeing b7, so that after **1. ... Qxa5 2. Qxb7** Black is also mated.
In the right part of the diagram the white queen protects against mate on h2. Black can remove the protection of h2 by **1. ... Rh5+ 2. Bxh5 Qh2#**.

In the diagram (⇨) the white queen is protecting the important squares d1 and e1. Interfering with **1. ... Nd1** is not very useful since White is not forced to capture the knight. He makes air for his king with **2. h3**. To win, Black must attack the queen as well: **1. ... Rd1+ 2. Bxd1 Re1#**.

The examples considered so far involve a combination of an interfering move and an attack on an important piece (including check). In each case, the interfering piece itself plays an active role. The diagram (⇩) shows two more examples although slightly different.
On the left the rook on d6 is no longer protected after **1. ... Nb4+ 2. cxb4**. Black makes use of a pin.
On the right the interfering move **1. ... Ng4** puts a stop to the queen's protection of e2. Since the knight on g4 is also attacking the bishop on f2. After this kind of double attack White will lose a piece.

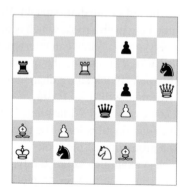

The interfering piece attacks nothing
In the following two examples, the interfering piece plays a passive role.

In the upper part of the diagram (⇧) the rooks are protecting each other, rendering the king's 'double attack' innocuous. After the interfering move **1. Nd7**, however, the double attack is all of a sudden effective and Black is powerless against the loss of at least an exchange.

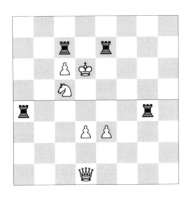

In the lower part of the diagram, too, Black cannot escape the loss of material. Here a simple pawn move (**1. e4** or **1. d4**) will cost a rook. This, then, is another example of a double attack that is made effective by means of interference.

The diagram (⇨) contains two positions. In each position, White sets up a combination with the help of an interfering move.
On the left, White wins with **1. c4+** (a discovered check). Rather than find a target, the front piece interferes with the protection the e4-rook is offering to the knight. White picks up the knight on a4 on the next move.
On the right, the interfering **1. Ng8** eliminates the defending queen and traps the rook on h8. Black will lose his rook.

Combining motives
In the diagram (⇩) the rook on c8 is an important defender. It protects the queen and prevents mate on the back rank. White can lure away the rook with 1. Qxc7, but after 1. ... Rxc7 the e8-square is still protected by the bishop on h5. White must therefore start with the powerful **1. Re8+!** After **1. ... Bxe8** the bishop interferes with the rook's defensive task, and so White can give mate with 2. Qf8#. Black can choose a slower death and accept the loss of material with 1. ... Rxe8, allowing 2. Qxc7. This, example,

then, involves a combination of eliminating the defender by luring away and interference.

In the diagram (⇧) the rook on f7 is the main defender. White can play 1. Nf5, but this move is not menacing enough; Black can bring his bishop into safety. The correct move is **1. Nf3** (interference). Once again the bishop is in danger and at the same time White is threatening a knight fork on e5. Black has to settle for a draw. If we put the black king on g8 then **1. Nf5** is the right move.

Search strategy

The search strategy for interfering moves is straightforward. Which pieces are being attacked? Is there a mate somewhere? The answer will lead to an important defender.

In the diagram (⇨) there are three defenders: the queen, the king and the rook. Black can try 1. … Ne3+ to chase away the king, but this yields nothing after 2. Rxe3 Qxe3 3. Qxh4+ or 3. d8Q. The queen turns out to be an essential defender, preventing mate on g2. Once this has been realised, the solution is obvious: Black can eliminate the defending queen with **1. … Ng3+**.

PRACTICE

Reminder
◊   *Elimination of the defence: interference*

Workbook

☐   *Elimination of the defence / Interfering: A*   ♖
   Explanation: In the exercises the students should look for important defenders. These can be found by looking for pieces that are attacked or by looking for a possible mate. By means of interfering the defender can be eliminated. Here, as in previous Steps, it is a good idea to ask the students to draw a circle round the defender, as this forces a direct approach.

Mistake:	The correct solution is not found.
Help:	Check whether the student, with the help of a new theme, understands the purpose of the exercise, e.g. by asking him which moves he has already tried. Let the student talk as much as possible.
Mistake:	The suggested solution to position 8 is 1. Ne2.
Help:	Ask the student to indicate the purpose of the knight move (1. ... Qxe2 2. Qf8+ or 1. ... Nxe2 2. Qxe8#). Which other possibilities does Black have? Ask the students to provide these themselves, or, if necessary, give the answer: after 1. ... Qxf1+ 2. Qxf1 Nxe2 the win is not quite there yet. The students should find this out for themselves; their main idea was correct, however. At this point, the correct 1. Ne4 will no longer be a problem.

☐ *Elimination of the defence / Interfering: B* ♜ ♜

Explanation: See exercise sheet A.

Mistake:	Position 11 is not solved.
Help:	The difficulty of this position lies in the fact that the bishop must be played to a square which is attacked three times and not defended at all. It is therefore hard to give help without giving hints. Supporting questions are: "Why is 1. Qb8+ insufficient?" (Besides protecting the queen, the c6-rook has another important function) "Where could the rook, with the aid of another piece, give mate?"
Mistake:	Position 12.
Help:	The attention is diverted by the attack on the white queen. If we disregard this attack and ask where White can give mate, then the solution is near. The queen on h3 covers the square c8, and although the interfering move 1. g4 puts the queen en prise one more time, it is nevertheless the right move.

ANSWERS

☐ *Elimination of the defence / Interfering: A*

1) 1. Nf5+ followed by 2. Rxh3.

2) 1. Nc6+ bxc6 2. Qxc5

3) 1. Bb8 and the rook on a8 is trapped.

4) 1. ... Nf4 (threatens 2. ... Ne2+) 2. exf4 Qxd6

5) 1. ... Nf3+ 2. gxf3 Qxd1+

6) 1. ... Be2 and White must give up an exchange.

7) 1. ... Bb5 2. axb5 Qxe2#

8) 1. Ne4 threatening 2. Qxe8 and 2. Rxe1. 1. ... Qxe4 is met by 2. Qf8+, mating. Less good is 1. Ne2, since Black can play on after

1. ... Qxf1+ 2. Qxf1 Nxe2.
9) 1. Rg6 fxg6 2. Qxg7#
10) 1. ... c4+ 2. Kh1 Qxb5
11) 1. Bc8 threatening 2. Bxb7 and 2.

Re8#. Not good is 1. Rc8+ Rxc8
2. Bxc8 Rb1.
12) 1. ... Rc1+ 2. Bxc1 2. Qb1#; 2.
Rxc1 Qxd5

☐ *Elimination of the defence / Interfering: B*
1) 1. ... Bb3 2. axb3 Nc2#
2) 1. ... Bc1+ 2. Kxc1 Qxg1
3) 1. ... Rc1+ 2. Nxc1 Qd1# or 2.
Rxc1 Qxb7
4) 1. d5 cxd5 2. Rg1+; 1. Rg1+ is
met by 1. ... Rg5.
5) Drawing
6) Drawing
7) 1. Rc6 dxc6 2. Nxf6+; bad is 1.
Nc6? Nxe4

8) 1. e6 fxe6 (1. ... Bxe6 2. Nxe6) 2.
Qxg4 (2. ... e5 3. Nf5 or 3. Ne6)
9) 1. ... Nf3+ 2. Kf1 Rxf6; 2. Rxf3
Rxh6
10) 1. Rd8+ Bxd8 2. Qe8# or 1. ...
Rxd8 2. Qxb7
11) 1. Bd6 Qxb3 2. Rf8#; 1. ... Rxd6
2. Qb8+; 1. ... Nxd6 2. Qxe6+
12) 1. g4 Qxf3 2. Rc8+ and mate

Information for the trainer
Interfering is often confused with interposing.
Note, however, that there is a difference: interfering eliminates the *defender*, while interposing
eliminates the *attacker*.

In the left part of the diagram White plays **1.
Bb3**, interposing the bishop, i.e. one of his own
pieces, between the attacker and the threatened
piece. Interfering involves placing one's own
piece between the defender and the threatened
piece, that is to say between two opposing pieces.

On the right Black plays **1. ... Nh4+**. Interfering
thus involves a fourth piece, in this case the
king on g2.

3   Luring

AIM OF THE LESSON
- learning tactical skills
- increasing the level of tactical skills

PRIOR KNOWLEDGE
- all types of double attack covered so far

ACQUISITION

Instruction
The tactical topics of Step 4 should be tackled only if the topics of previous Steps have been mastered sufficiently. The combinations considered so far have not been deeper than one and a half moves. In this Step we will consider the kind of moves that are required before a combination can itself be executed. Such moves are called **preparatory moves**. In this Step we will look at five different types of preparatory moves. First of all we will discuss the concept of **luring** in combination with the double attack.

Exchanging
Luring is effective when the defending side still has a defence against a double attack. In the diagram (⇨) the fork 1. Nd5 does not work on account of 1. ... Qxb3. White first has to lure or entice another piece to the b6-square with a capture so as to get the double attack to work: **1. Qxb6+ Kxb6 2. Nd5+** winning the rook.

In the diagram (⇩) the double attack 1. Be5 does not work on account of 1. ... Rd3+ or 1. ... Rxg2. The solution is straightforward. White first exchanges rooks on g7 and then wins the rook on d4: **1. Rxg7+ Kxg7 2. Be5+**.

25

In these examples the double attack works only in combination with a preceding preparatory move.

A direct attack on an identical piece is usually ineffective. In such cases, luring can be the solution. The diagram (⇧) contains two positions in which the piece that has to mount the double attack would, without a preparatory move, be captured. On the left 1. Nb5 would be premature, but after **1. Bxd6 Kxd6 2. Nb5+** picks up a piece.

On the right, Black has to prepare g5 by first capturing on h4. After **1. ... Nxh4 2. Rxh4 g5** Black wins a piece.

In both cases, a piece is lured to a fatal square by means of an exchange.

Reversing the order of moves

When a certain move order does not work, luring sometimes does the trick. In the left part of the diagram (⇨), attacking the pinned knight with 1. ... Nc4 does not give Black anything, since White has everything under control after 2. Bc3. Again, Black must resort to a preparatory luring move: **1. ... Bxb2+ 2. Kxb2 Nc4+.** Reversing the order of moves is often worth a try.

On the right, 1. Qh5+ does not win a piece because of the defence 1. ... Nf7. By exchanging on h6 first this problem can be solved: **1. Bxh6 Bxh6 2. Qh5+.**

A sacrifice

In addition to exchanging, luring can also be done by means of a sacrifice.

In the diagram (⇩) we see two simple examples. On the left, White plays **1. Ra8+ Kxa8 2. Nb6+**, winning material.

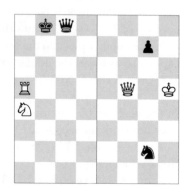

On the right, Black uncorks the surprising **1. ... g6+**. White loses his queen, no matter how he captures on g6: **2. Qxg6 Nf4+** or **2. Kxg6 Nh4+.**

The word 'luring' suggests that there is a choice. This is, however, not always the case. In the two positions in the diagram (⇧) the losing side does not have a choice. Yet, we refer to these cases as examples of luring.

On the left, White wins a piece with **1. Qa8+ Kxa8** (only move) **2. Nxb6+.**

On the right, Black wins the knight with **1. ... f2+ 2. Kxf2 Qh4+** (not 2. ... Qf6+ 3. Nf3).

Exploiting pins

Double attacks frequently involve pins. In the upper part of the diagram (⇨) the black bishop is pinned. White can exploit this with the help of a preparatory move: **1. Rd8 Rxd8 2. Bxf6+**, winning material. Black can limit the damage to the loss of an exchange with **1. ... Kg7 2. Rxf8 Bxe5**.

In the lower part of the diagram the pin comes one move later: **1. ... Rxf1+ 2. Kxf1 Ne3+**. Black wins the queen, since the now pinned knight on g2 is no longer defending the e3-square.

This concludes our discussion of luring for the moment. The remainder of the lesson on the different forms of the double attack can be discussed at a later stage.

Summing up, we have seen that luring attracts a target (the king or another piece) to a particular square by means of an exchange or a sacrifice, after which a double attack becomes possible.

The discovered attack

In the diagram (⇩) we see a battery of rook and knight that is ready to strike. However, as things stand, there is as yet no forcing discovered attack; after 1. Nc5 bxc5 2. Bxe7+ White has not won any material. The trick is to first lure the king to e7. After **1. Bxe7+ Kxe7** (it is better to move the king away) **2. Nc5+** the battery does

27

work, and White wins the queen with the help of a discovered check.

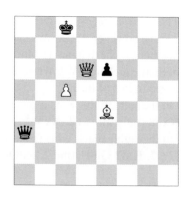

In the diagram (⇧) the sacrifice **1. Bb7+** lures the black king to a fatal square. After **1. ... Kxb7 2. c6+** White wins the queen.

The next two examples involve luring of 'material'. In the left part of the diagram (⇨) we see an as yet ineffective battery of a queen on c6 and a pawn on b5. **1. Ra4** lures the black queen to a4. White can then wrap up with **1. ... Qxa4 2. b6+**. White has to start with a rook sacrifice, because after 1. b6+ Qxb6 2. Ra4+ Black escapes with 2. … Na5.

On the right, Black can win a pawn with 1. ... Bg5+. However, he can go after bigger prey by attracting the queen with the move **1. ... Rxe3+**. After **2. Qxe3**, Black wins the queen with either **2. … Bg5+** or **2. … Bf2+**.

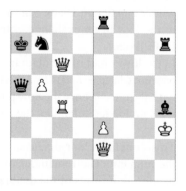

A preparatory move that involves luring picks out a target, which is subsequently eliminated with the help of a double attack. Luring moves can target both the king and other pieces. Luring can form part of all types of double attack. If there is enough time (and concentration!), we can conclude this lesson by looking at an endgame study of Rinck. This study is characterised by a series of preparatory moves that involve luring by means of X-ray checks.

In the diagram (⇩) White wins after **1. Ra8 Qxa2 2. Rxa4 Qg8 3. Ra8 Qh7 4. Bg6 Qxg6 5. Ra6+**.

Magnificent. The queen is lured from one square to the next, until it has no place left to go. It is a good idea to ask the students to indicate the squares to which the queen can and cannot go after each move. Note that throughout the rook and the bishop are indirectly protected on account of the X-ray checks on f3, e8, f3 and a6.

Reminder

◊   *Double attack: luring*

Workbook

☐ *Double attack: Luring: A*   ♖

Explanation: The search strategy for double attacks with the knight is straightforward. All pieces within the knight's range are natural targets
(but only unprotected pieces, pieces of a higher value and the
king). One of the pieces is already within range; a second piece
must be lured there. In each of the positions the enemy king has
an important role to play.

Mistake: The correct solution is not found.

Help: This is not a good sign! The student must focus on the knight.
What are the possibilities? Which pieces can the knight attack,
and which pieces can the knight not attack, at least not for the
time being. Lure a piece to the correct square.

Mistake: The pins in positions 9, 11 and 12 cause problems.

Help: An obvious, but undesirable, solution is to simplify the positions
by removing or replacing pieces. Establish whether the student
has the basic skills required to exploit pins. If not, revision of the
exercises that deal with the theme 'a pinned piece is not a good
defender' is required.

☐ *Double attack: Luring: B*   ♖

Explanation: The search strategy for double attacks of the queen should focus
on unprotected pieces.

Mistake: The positions in which the target is mate are not found (i.e. positions 6, 7, 8 and 12).

Help: The answer to the question "Where could you give mate with
the queen?" usually leads to the correct answer. In most cases,
only one mate is possible.

Mistake: The order of moves is wrong (positions 3, 5 and 8).

Help: Put the suggested solution on the board and ask the student to
look for a defence. After this another try is in order.

☐ *Double attack: Luring: C*   ♖ ♖

Explanation: Each of the positions contains a battery. Unfortunately, the battery
is ineffective, since the main piece does not yet have a suitable

target. A discovered attack or discovered check must be prepared with the help of a luring move.

Mistake: The answer is wrong.

Help: Point out the battery. "Do you see an attacking target for the front piece?"

Mistake: A defence is missed (e.g. 1. Nxd6 Qe3+ in position 3 or 1. ... Rxf1+ 2. Kxf1 Bb5+ 3. Rxb5 in position 9).

Help: Play the suggested move and then ask what the opponent can play now.

☐ *Double attack: Luring: D*   ♖ ♖ ♖

Explanation: This exercise sheet contains other types of double attacks (with pawns, bishops and rooks), X-ray checks and X-ray attacks. These are more difficult since the search strategy is more extensive. In the case of pawn forks two pieces occupy the same file with one square between them. To make an X-ray check or X-ray attack possible, two enemy pieces have to be lured on to the same line. For double attacks of rook and bishop it is important that the enemy pieces end up on the same file, rank or diagonal. It is also possible to do this exercise sheet at a later point during the training.

Mistake: The suggested solution is incorrect.

Help: Set up the position, play the wrong move and ask the student to comment on his suggestion. Direct the student to the correct answer with the help of questions.

ANSWERS

☐ *Double attack: Luring: A*

1) 1. ... Rd2+ 2. Qxd2 Nf3+
2) 1. Qxf6+ Kxf6 2. Ne4+
3) 1. Qxc6 Qxc6 2. Nxe7+
4) Drawing
5) Drawing
6) 1. Bh6+ Kxh6 2. Nf7+; 1. ... Kh8 2. Nf7#
7) 1. Qh8+ Kxh8 2. Nxg6+ and 3. Nxe7
8) 1. Bxf7+ Kxf7 (better 1. ... Kd8)

2. Ne5+
9) 1. ... Qxg3+ 2. Kxg3 Ne4+ and 3. ... Nxd2
10) 1. ... Bg5 2. Qxg5 Nh3+
11) 1. ... Rc1 2. Qxc1 Ne2+
12) 1. Qxf8+ Kxf8 2. Ne6+ and 3. Nxd8; 1. Ne6? Qxe7 or 1. Bxg7 Nxg7 2. Qxg7+ and 3. Ne6+ only wins an exchange.

Double attack: Luring: B

1) 1. ... Rxg2+ 2. Kxg2 Qe4+ and 3. … Qxb1
2) 1. ... Rxf1+ 2. Kxf1 Qd1+ 3. Kg2 Qxg4+
3) 1. Bxf7+ Kxf7 2. Qd5+; 1. Qd5? Qe7
4) 1. ... Rxg2+ 2. Kxg2 Qg5+
5) 1. Nd7 Rxd7 2. Qh3+; 1. Qh3+? Kg7 2. Nd7 Qd6 3. Nxb8 Rh8
6) 1. d5 Bxd5 2. Qd4
7) 1. Rxd6 Rxd6 2. Qe5
8) 1. ... Rxd4 2. Rxd4 Qe5
9) 1. Rxb7 Rxb7 2. Qa8+ or 1. Rxe7 Qxg2#
10) 1. ... Rxa5 2. Rxa5 Qe1+
11) 1. Bxa6 Rxa6 2. Qd3
12) 1. b4 Bxb4 2. Qd4

Double attack: Luring: C

1) 1. Rf8+ Kxf8 2. Bxg7+
2) 1. Bb7+ Kxb7 2. c6+
3) 1. Qxh7+ Kxh7 2. Nxd6+; 1. Nxd6? Qe3+
4) 1. ... Qxg2+ 2. Kxg2 d4+; 1. … d4 2. Qd2 or 2. Qc4+
5) 1. ... Rxf1+ 2. Kxf1 Bh3+ (2. … Bd3+ 3. Nxd3)
6) 1. ... Nxd4 2. Qxd4? Ng4+
7) 1. Rd7+ Kxd7 (1. … Ke6 2. Qd5#) 2. Nxf6+
8) 1. Rd4 Qxd4 2. e6+
9) 1. ... Rxf1+ 2. Kxf1 Bxg2+! (2. … Bb5+ 3. Rxb5)
10) 1. Rxd7 Qxd7 2. Nh6+
11) 1. ... Qd3+ 2. Kxd3 Bxc6+
12) 1. Bxc5 Qxc5 2. axb4

Double attack: Luring: D

1) 1. Nxe5 Rxe5 2. f4 (double attack: pawn)
2) 1. Rb8 Rxb8 2. Bxe5+ (double attack: bishop)
3) 1. Rg8+ Qxg8 2. Rg2+ (X-ray check)
4) 1. Rxd3 Rxd3 2. Be4 (double attack: 2 pieces)
5) Drawing
6) 1. Qc4+ Qxc4 2. g8Q+ (X-ray check)
7) 1. ... Nxc2 2. Qxc2 Bxd3+ (double attack: bishop)
8) 1. ... Qxf1+ 2. Kxf1 Rxf5+ (double attack: rook)
9) 1. Be7 Qxe7 2. f6 (double attack: 2 pieces)
10) 1. Qxd7 Qxd7 2. Bxe6+ (double attack: bishop)
11) 1. ... Rxc4 2. Qxc4 Bd5 (X-ray attack)
12) 1. Bc4+ Kf8 2. Rxe8+; 1. Rxe8? Rxa6+ (double attack: bishop)

4 Blocking

AIM OF THE LESSON
- learning a new attacking weapon

PRIOR KNOWLEDGE
- different forms of eliminating the defender

ACQUISITION

Instruction
The four forms of eliminating the defender (i.e. capturing, chasing away, luring and interfering) discussed so far are all means to achieve a goal, such as winning material or giving mate.
In blocking, the goal of mate is particularly relevant. Sometimes blocking is also useful when cashing in on passed pawns (see lesson 7).

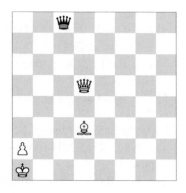

Blocking by giving check
The diagram (⇨) contains a straightforward example. Black does not appear to have enough pieces to give mate. After a check on c3 the king flees to b1 and after a check on c1 White puts the bishop on b1. However, once the bishop is on b1 the white king cannot go there anymore. Thus, Black plays **1. ... Qc1+ 2. Bb1 Qc3#**. The b1-square is blocked by the bishop.
In the diagram (⇩) the black king has only one square available, after 1. Rh8+, i.e. f7. After **1. Be6+** Black does not have much of a choice: **1. ... Bf7**. He has to block the flight square, allowing White to give mate with **2. Rh8#**.
Both examples involve the same scenario: first a check, then the defender gets out of check by interposing a piece. Next, the attacker gives mate since the king's flight square is now blocked by the piece he himself has interposed.

Luring

In the diagram (⇑) we see another kind of blocking. The first thing we notice is that the piece that must give mate, the queen, is also guarding the flight square on f7. That is why after 1. Qh7+ the black king simply moves to f7. White must resort to a pawn sacrifice to block the escape route: **1. f7+ Qxf7 2. Qh7#**. The queen is lured to f7 where it blocks the king.

In the diagram (⇨) 1. ... Qg4+ 2. Kf1 does not give Black anything (other than a repetition of moves). However, blocking the f1-square allows a pretty mate: **1. ... f1Q+ 2. Qxf1 Qg4#**. Here, too, both examples involve the same scenario: first the attacker gives check using a sacrifice, then the defender gets out of the check by accepting the sacrifice, and then the attacker gives mate because the flight square of the king is blocked.

Smothered mate

A special kind of blocking is the smothered mate. In a smothered mate a knight gives mate with all the squares surrounding the king being occupied by the king's own pieces. From the initial position, a smothered mate arises after **1. e4 c6 2. d4 d5 3. Nc3 dxe4 4. Nxe4 Nd7 5. Qe2 Ngf6?? 6. Nd6#**. The e-pawn is pinned, and so Black is mated. This mate is possible only because of a horrible blunder on the part of the opponent.

In some cases, blocking can be used to force a smothered mate. The basic position is shown in the diagram (⇩). It is fun to have the children look for the solution. The mate is easy to spot only if this type of position has been encountered before. The right approach is **1. Nf7+ Kg8 2. Nh6+** (double check) **2. ... Kh8** (or 2. ... Kf8 3. Qf7 mate) **3. Qg8+ Rxg8 4. Nf7#**. Crucially, the f7-square is not protected by a black piece.

The upper part of the diagram (⇧) contains the same mating position, but here an extra finesse is required: **1. Nf7+ Kg8** and the rest is familiar. If Black plays **1. ... Rxf7** then **2. Qxc8+** wraps things up.

In the bottom part of the diagram White is in trouble after **1. ... Qd4+** (wrong is 1. ... Qe3+ 2. Kh1 Nf2+ 3. Rxf2) **2. Kh1 Nf2+**. The rook cannot take the knight because it must protect its colleague on a1. The story after **3. Kg1** has been told before: **3. ... Nh3+ 4. Kh1 Qg1+ 5. Rxg1 Nf2#**.

There is a quicker version of the smothered mate. In the diagram (⇨) the white bishop on d5 lends a helping hand: **1. Qg8+ Rxg8 2. Nf7#** leads to a direct mate. Now 1. Nf7+ Rxf7 only nets an exchange. Note that here the rook on c8 is protected.

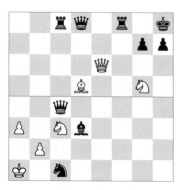

In the lower part of the diagram there is no smothered mate, although the parallels are clear. Black cashes in with **1. ... Qa2+ 2. Nxa2 Nb3#**. 1. ... Nb3+ 2. Ka2 is nothing but a loss of time; there is nothing better than to start over again with 2. ... Nc1+.

Combining motives
Blocking can also go hand in hand with other combinations. The first example that we consider involves a combination of blocking and eliminating the defender.

In the left part of the diagram (⇩) White can win with **1. Rc8+**. Black can choose the combination that will finish him off: **1. ... Qxc8 2. Qa7#** (blocking) or **1. ... Kxc8 2. Qa8#** (luring away + mate).

On the right, Black lures the queen away from the defence of g3 with **1. ... Rf1+**. After **2. Qxf1 Rxf1+ 3. Rxf1 Qxg3#** it is mate. Another example of luring away + mate.

Another combination is that of blocking and double attack.
In the upper part of the diagram (⇧) White plays the strong **1. b5+**. Black can take the pawn in two ways. If Black captures with the king we have an example of 'luring' as discussed in the previous lesson. After **1. ... Kxb5 2. Nd4+** loses the queen. The other capture leads to a mate that involves blocking: **1. ... Qxb5+ 2. Nb8#**. In the lower part of the diagram we see a similar motif. Black can ignore the fact that his rook is hanging and win with **1. ... f2+**. After **2. Qxf2** (2. Kf1 Bd3+) **2. ... Rh1#** the queen blocks f2; after **2. Kxh2** Black decides matters with promotion to a minor piece: **2. ... f1N+**.

In the diagram (⇨) the battery on the second rank stands out. An obvious try is 1. Bd1+, winning the queen. However, it turns out that the position is more difficult than would appear at first sight, since after 1. ... Kh6 2. Rxg2 it is stalemate. White must therefore find another target for the front piece. With the surprising discovered attack **1. Bg6+** White wins with the help of the blockade: **1. ... Qxg6** (otherwise White simply takes the queen) **2. Rh2#**.

Dessert
We will conclude this lesson by discussing two pretty examples in which the attacking side can give mate only after sacrificing material. Both are admittedly difficult, but they never fail to be appreciated.
In the diagram (⇩) the students must first look for themselves. After a while they will come to the solution 1. Rf4+ Bxf4 2. e4+. An understandable mistake; in the initial position the g4-square is under control, but after the rook sacrifice it is no longer the case. White has to block two squares in front of the black king. This can be achieved with **1. g4+ Nxg4 2. Rf4+ Bxf4 3. e4#**.

In the diagram (⇧) 1. Rxg5+ Rxg5 2. Nf4+ does not lead to mate, since the g4-square becomes available to the black king. For the win White must sacrifice no fewer than 11 points: **1. Rh4+ gxh4 2. g4+ Bxg4 3. Rg5+ Rxg5 4. Nf4#.**

Search strategy

In the exercises (which are much easier than the two previous examples) the students have to look for mate. The flight squares of the king can be taken away by means of blocking.

In the diagram (⇨) the g7-bishop prevents the queen from giving mate on e5. Moving the bishop to c3 does not work, since then White (after 2. Qe5+) loses control of h6. With the blocking **1. Bh6+** White can give a forced mate: **1. … Rxh6 2. Qe5#.**

PRACTICE

Reminder
◊   *Elimination of the defence: blocking*

Workbook

□ *Elimination of the defence / Blocking: A* ♖
    Explanation: The side that is to move can win in the attack by blocking the opposing king's flight squares. The exercise is correct when material has been gained or mate has been given.
    Mistake: The king can still escape.
    Help: Usually the students have omitted the blocking move. Ask the students to look at the position from the opponent's perspective. Which flight square does the king still have? How can this flight square be taken away?
    Mistake: "This assignment is impossible. I don't see a mate."
    Help: In the positions 7, 11 and 12 the solution does not lead to a forced mate. Point out that there is a forced gain of material, however.
    Mistake: The positions 7 and 12 cannot be solved.
    Help: The first move is a 'quiet' move (i.e. not a capture or check).

□ *Elimination of the defence / Blocking: B* ♖♖

Explanation: See exercises sheet A.
Mistake: Position 6 is not found.
Help: The first move is a 'quiet' move (i.e. not a capture or check). Position 6 involves a combination of luring and blocking. The rook on f8 must be made to disappear (1. Nf7+ Rxf7 obviously leads to nothing). How? It can only be achieved with 1. Bg8.
Mistake: The suggested solution in position 10 is 1. ... Rh5 or 1. ... Qxh2+.
Help: The students should find out for themselves why the answer is wrong. (2. Qg7# and 2. Kxh2 Rh5+ 3. Kg3, respectively). Why is the queen sacrifice ineffective? Because the king can escape. Using this lesson's subject matter, it seems a good idea to block the g3-square. The students will refrain from playing this on account of 2. Rxg3, but in that case 2. ... Re1+ 3. Rg1 Qg2# follows.

ANSWERS

□ *Elimination of the defence / Blocking: A*
1) 1. e7+ Rxe7 2. Qh8#   Rxb2
2) 1. Qxd5+ Qf7 2. Rh8#   8) 1. Qg7+ Nxg7 2. Nh6#
3) 1. Qb8+ Rxb8 2. Nc7#   9) 1. Rh3+ Bxh3 2. g3#
4) 1. ... Rd1+ 2. Qxd1 Qf2#; 2. Kxd1   10) 1. ... Rf1+ 2. Qxf1 Qe3#; 2. Kxf1
   Qxf1#   Qe1#
5) 1. d6+ Rxd6 2. Bh4#   11) 1. ... e5+ 2. dxe5 Qd2#; 2. Kxe5
6) 1. Qg8+ Rxg8 2. Nf7#; 1. Nf7+   Qxg3+
   Rxf7 does not win.   12) 1. Re7 Rxe7 2. Qh7+; 1. ... g6 2.
7) 1. ... Rg2 2. Qxg2 Qh5#; 2. Qd1   Rxd7

□ *Elimination of the defence / Blocking: B*
1) 1. ... Rg1+ 2. Bxg1 Qe2#   8) 1. Rf4+ Kh5 2. Rh4+ gxh4 3. g4#
2) 1. Qe7+ Rxe7 2. Nf6#; 1. Nc7+?   9) 1. Qh7+ Nxh7 2. Ng6+ Kg8 3.
   Qxc7   Bd5#
3) 1. Rh8+ Nxh8 2. Bh7#   10) 1. ... g3 2. fxg3 Qxh2+ 3. Kxh2
4) 1. Ne7+ Nxe7 2. Rxf8+ Kxf8 3.   Rh5#; 2. Rxg3 Re1+ 3. Rg1 Qg2#
   Rd8#   11) 1. ... Bxf3+ 2. Bxf3 Be5; 1. ...
5) 1. Rf8+ Rxf8 2. Ng7#   Be5? 2. f4
6) 1. Bg8 Rxg8 2. Nf7#   12) 1. ... Rf2+ 2. Rxf2 Qh5+ 3. Kg1
7) 1. Rf8+ Qxf8 2. Rxf8+ Rxf8 3.   Qh1
   Qxg6#

37

5

Thinking ahead

AIM OF THE LESSON
- practising visualisation skills

PRIOR KNOWLEDGE
- thinking ahead
- visualisation

ACQUISITION

Instruction
This lesson is entirely devoted to the skill of
visualisation, which is an essential part of thinking ahead. We will consider and evaluate a
position by investigating a number of different
continuations, with some clever moves along
the way. The set-up of this training session is
as follows:

Each student sets up the position in the diagram (⇨) on his own board. After this, no one
is allowed to touch the pieces, except when told
to do so by the trainer.
We begin by asking which starting move the
students have in mind. It is important to involve
everyone in this. So, we ask each of the students
individually which move they would play, even
though it is likely that the same move will be
suggested more than once. The suggested moves
include **1. h3**, **1. Qe2**, **1. Qd2**, **1. Re1**, **1. Qd3**,
1. Bf2, and **1. Nd5**. The move **1. h3** is clearly
ill-conceived, since it runs into **1. ... Ne3**. Do
not say this but ask the students what he expects
Black to play next. The student should ideally
provide the correct counter move himself. The
other moves suggest that the threat of 1. ... Ne3
has been spotted. These moves, while not bad,
are a bit too defensive.

After a brief discussion we come to the best move, **1. Nd5**, and ask the students what they expect Black's next move to be.
A popular choice after **1. Nd5** is **1. … Qc5+**, when we arrive at the diagram (⇧). Without touching the pieces, the students now have to come up with a move for White. Here many will go for **2. Bf2** or **2. Kh1**. We then ask the students to find a reply to **2. Kh1**, e.g. **2. ... Bf8**. What is crucial is that the students acknowledge that the bishop is in danger. After **2. Bf2** the students should see that the queen is under attack, and that **2. ... Nxf2** is now possible. After every move we stop and take stock, asking questions such as:

- What is White's / Black's plan?
- Are any of the pieces in danger?
- Do you see another good move?

These questions direct the students' thinking and guide them in the direction of the salient aspects of the position.
On the 3rd move, after **1. Nd5 Qc5+ 2. Bf2 Nxf2** (see diagram ⇨), the students will now find **3. Rxf2** and **3. Nxe7+**. After **3. Rxf2** we check whether the bishop on e7 has been taken into consideration. The chances are that this is the case, given that this threat was already pointed out earlier. **3. Nxe7+** has to be followed by **3. ... Kf8**, which we check to be sure. In the main variation the students will now put forward moves like **4. Rxf2** and **4. Ng6+**. After capturing with the rook, Black captures on e7 with his king. We end by asking the students to evaluate the resulting position (material is still equal).
An interesting line is **4. Ng6+ fxg6 5. Rxf2** (diagram ⇩). Any other move will run into a smothered mate, as shown in the previous lesson. It is important to pause at each move so as to allow the students to take stock. It is also important to avoid making the lesson too long or complex, since this will put too much strain on the students' visualisation skills.

39

Throughout, we must realise that the aim of this lesson is for the students to visualise and discover possibilities, without directly looking for the best move. This means that the students are training their memory, and so the following points are important:

- Concentration is required, and so silence is in order (sit down yourself if necessary).
- Discipline. Name the moves clearly and slowly, listen to each other, follow each other's thoughts and build on these if and where needed.
- Repeat the moves to prevent confusion and to guarantee that everyone is working on the same position.
- Give moves only, no comments. Keep the variations as sparse as possible to avoid burdening the students' memory with irrelevant information.
- Make sure that there is sufficient time; at the end, make sure to evaluate the entire sequence of moves played.

It is clear that this kind of exercise draws heavily on the trainer's chess skills. Note that it is possible to differentiate by having the students look further and further ahead. If a student cannot follow a particular line, then he can execute some moves on his board, thus familiarizing himself with the position once more. It is also possible to vary the number of moves.

The present lesson is not accompanied by a separate practice sheet. This is therefore a good opportunity to practise and repeat some exercises from previous lessons. It is always a good idea to discuss an example together with the correct solution strategy. Ask the students to approach the position from a general point of view, rather than by looking for the right move straight away.

Useful questions include:
- Can I give check (mate)?
- Which pieces are unprotected?
- Which pieces are on the same line (file, rank or diagonal)?
- Which pieces are important defenders?

The important thing is what the students do with this information. For instance, unprotected pieces invite double attacks, while important defenders can be eliminated.

The following diagram (⇧) can be used as an example. Black, who is a piece behind, is to move.

The battery on the g-file is the secret of Black's success, but is not directly decisive. The solution is **1. ... Ne5 2. Nh4 Nf3+**. The reason why search strategies are of the utmost importance is that this type of position contains many seductive moves which may not work (e.g. 1. ... Nf4? 2. Qxf6).

Workbook

□ *Test / Mix:*

Explanation: The themes of lessons 2, 3 and 4 (interfering, luring and blocking) return in these exercises. This information makes it easier to find the correct answer.

Mistake: The correct solution is not found.

Help: The students should correct their own mistakes, if at all possible. This can be done by asking general questions such as "Which targets do you see?" and "Do you see an important defender?" If this fails, it is possible to reveal the theme of the exercise.

Mistake: The suggested answer is wrong.

Help: Look up the pointers in the relevant lesson. The themes of the exercises are given under the heading answers below.

□ *Test / Mix:*

Explanation: This exercise sheet contains the same themes as the A-sheet.

☐ *Test / Mix: C*

1) 1. Rd7+ Nxd7 2. Qg7#; 1. ... Qxd7 2. Nf6+ (interfering and double attack: luring)
2) 1. Nf6 Bxf6 2. Qe4; 1. ... gxf4 2. Rxh7# (blocking)
3) 1. ... b4 2. Bxb4 Qb7+; 1. ... Qb7+? 2. Qf3 (double attack: luring)
4) 1. ... Qxc3+ 2. Kxc3 Nxe4+ (double attack: luring)
5) 1. ... Rxd4 2. Qxd4 Ng4+ (discovered attack: luring)
6) 1. ... Rh4+ 2. Nxh4 g4#
7) 1. Rxb2 Rxb2 2. Qc3 (double attack: luring)
8) 1. R1e6 Bxe6 2. Qxh6; 1. ... Qxe6 2. Rxe6 Bxe6 3. Qxh6 f6 4. Qg6+ (interfering)
9) 1. ... Ra2+ 2.Bxa2 Nc2# (blocking)
10) 1. ... Bxc2+ 2. Kxc2 b3+ (discovered attack: luring)
11) 1. Nd5 exd5 2. Rxe7; 1. ... Rxd7 2. Nxe7+ or 1. ... Qxd7 2. Nxf6+ (interfering)
12) 1. Bc7 Rxc7 2. Qe5 (double attack: luring)

☐ *Test / Mix: D*

1) 1. ... Rd2 and 2. ... Nxf3+ (double attack: luring)
2) 1. Rh8+ Bxh8 2. Qxf7#; 1. ... Kxh8 2. Nxf7+ (luring away + mate or double attack: luring)
3) 1. Rxd4 Rxd4 2. Qe3 (double attack: luring)
4) 1. Qg7+ Kxg7 2. Rxg6# (discovered check: luring)
5) 1. Rxf6+ Kxf6 2. Qf2+ (double attack: luring)
6) 1. Qxd6 Kxd6 2. Bf4+ (discovered attack: luring)
7) 1. Qh7+ Nxh7 2. Ng6# (blocking)
8) 1. e7 Nxe7 2. Qc7 (double attack: luring)
9) 1. Qa4+ Ra5 2. Qc6+ Bb6 3. Qc8# (blocking)
10) 1. Qd5+ Qxd5 2. Nxe7+ (double attack: luring)
11) 1. ... Ne3 2. Nxd6 Qxd3+; 2. Qxe3 Qxd3+; 1. ... Nc3+? 2. Kc2 (interfering)
12) 1. Qxh7+ Kxh7 2. Nf5+ Kg8 3. Rxg7# (discovered check: luring)

6 The pin: luring

AIM OF THE LESSON
• improving tactical skills

PRIOR KNOWLEDGE
• all forms of the pin
• luring

ACQUISITION

Instruction
This course distinguishes three pin-related themes, i.e. 'the pin', 'attack on a pinned piece' and 'a pinned piece is not a good defender'. The exercise sheets of Step 2 and 3 provide enough material to test the students' knowledge and, if need be, to refresh their memory. Mirroring and changing the colour provides a 'new' position.

Luring the front piece + pin
For pins, preparatory moves often involve positioning the front or the back piece. It is therefore important to spot opportunities for (re)positioning front and back pieces. The way in which we cover this topic is similar to how we covered the preparatory move in relation to double attacks.
In the diagram (⇨) Black's bishop and his king are placed on the same diagonal, but White cannot exploit this straight away. However, by exchanging on d6 White can position a knight as the front piece. After **1. Nxd6 Nxd6 2. Be5** nets a piece.
In the diagram (⇩) Black lures the bishop to the f-file with the help of a sacrifice, where it ends up as the front piece of a pin: **1. ... f5 2. Bxf5 Rf8**.

Luring the front piece + attack on a pinned piece.
The diagram (⇧) already contains a pin. The bishop on b6 is pinned, but it is also adequately defended. Attacking the bishop with 1. a5 is met by 1. ... Bxc5. The problem is that the front and pinning piece are attacking each other. For this reason White must replace the present one with another front piece, with **1. Rxb6+ Rxb6**, after which **2. a5** wins material.

The example on the right is more difficult. Black first positions the front piece by giving check.
1. ... Qe4+ 2. Qg2 (2. Rg2 Re1+). Next, Black attacks the pinned queen once more with **2. ... Rd2**. White cannot capture on e4 on account of the mate on h2.

Giving check and forcing the opponent to get out of check by interposing is a useful weapon to lure a piece into a pin.

In the diagram (⇨) White seems to have everything under control. The only way in which Black can exploit the pinned bishop is by replacing it with another front piece by means of a sacrifice. What is more, he can deal out a surprising blow with **1. ... Qxb2+ 2. Qxb2 Rxc1#**. The queen is now pinned and so has lost its protective function.

Luring the front piece + a pinned piece is not a good defender
In the diagram (⇩) there is no pin yet. The bishop on f7 has to protect the knight on h5. With **1. g6** White closes off the diagonal of the bishop. If the bishop moves, White plays **2. Bxh5**. No matter how Black captures on g6, he will end up in a pin on the g-file: **1. ... fxg6** (or 1. ... Bxg6) **2. Bxh5**.

We have used three ways of luring so far:
• exchanging a piece
• a sacrifice
• a check to position the interposing piece

Another type of preparatory move is a luring move which positions the back piece creating the opportunity to exploit the pin. The three pin-related themes, i.e. 'the pin', 'attack on a pinned piece' and 'a pinned piece is not a good defender' will pop up again.

Luring the back piece + pin
The left part of the diagram (⇧) offers a straight-forward example. White first plays **1. Rxb8+** so as to pin the bishop after **1. ... Kxb8 2. Rb1**. On the right, White plays **1. g8Q+**. After **1. ... Kxg8, 2. Bd5** wins the jackpot. Note that White cannot do anything without first luring the king on to g8, since the direct 1. Bd5 is met by 1. ... Rh6+ or 1. ... Re2+.

Luring the back piece + attack on a pinned piece
In the left part of the diagram (⇨) 1. ... c5 does not achieve anything because the bishop on d5 is hanging (2. Nxd5). However, after the exchange **1. ... Bxb3 2. Qxb3** Black has managed to put in place a back piece. He can exploit the resulting pin with **2. ... c5**.

On the right, the knight on f5 is only parti-ally pinned, since it can still move to e7 or h4. This means that attacking it with 1. g4 is as yet ineffective. White can win material by first exchanging on g6: **1. Nxg6 Kxg6 2. g4**, winning a piece.

Luring the back piece + a pinned piece is not a good defender.
In the diagram (⇩) the bishop on d6 is pinned. Still, 1. Qxc5 Bxc5+ does not give White any-thing. After **1. Bxd7+**, however, the king is lured to d7, and now that the king is the back piece, the pin can be exploited. The bishop is no longer protecting the queen, which White is therefore free to take with **2. Qxc5.**

In the diagram (⇧) White appears to be fine. But all that glitters is not gold: Black, with the help of a pretty rook sacrifice, has a mate in three: **1. ... Rh1+ 2. Kxh1** (the back piece has been placed) **2. ... Qxh3+ 3. Kg1 Qxg2#.**

Search strategy

The search strategy for the exercise sheets focuses first and foremost on the existing pin. The correct move makes the front or the back piece vulnerable, by means of an exchange or a sacrifice. Defending pieces can suddenly lose their protective function because they end up as front or back piece.

The positions in which there is as yet no pin present are more difficult. An example is shown in the diagram (⇨). White is two pawns behind, and so 1. Rxa5 is definitely not sufficient. A strong move is **1. Rc7+**. The king cannot go to the back rank on account of the pin on c8 (i.e. 1. ... Kg8 2. Rc8). Black can do little more than interpose his rook on d7. This rook has become the front piece, and all White has to do is to attack it one more time with **2. Qb5.**

Reminder
◊ *Pin: placing the front and back piece*

Workbook

☐ *Pin / Placing the back piece: A*   ♖
Explanation: The back piece has to be lured to the correct square by means of an exchange or a sacrifice. The students should spot existing pins first; as a consequence, these exercises are relatively straightforward. In those positions in which there is no pin present yet, one has to be put in place, again by means of an exchange or a sacrifice. In the exercises with the theme 'pin' the students

should focus on unprotected and (relatively) valuable pieces. In the exercises with the theme 'a pinned piece is not a good defender' the students should focus on protected pieces. All in all, this is a fairly difficult exercise sheet.

If necessary, the trainer can give away the arrangement of the exercise sheet:
- 4x luring the back piece + pin
- 4x luring the back piece + attack on a pinned piece
- 4x luring the back piece + a pinned piece is not a good defender.

Mistake: The order of moves is wrong (positions 2, 3, 5, 6, 10, 12)

Help: The right solution is not far off. Ask the students to find out the cause of their mistakes themselves. How can this defence be prevented? This can be done by reversing the move order! Below, the wrong moves are given together with the answers.

Mistake: Position 8 is not solved correctly.

Help: There is no pin yet, and therefore nothing concrete to go on. Still, there is not a lot White can do on account of his hanging queen. Giving check is the only option. Asking the right questions should help the students find the right move.

☐ *Pin / Placing the front piece: A*   ♖

Explanation: The front piece has to be lured to the correct square with an exchange or a sacrifice. The students should first look for pins that are already present. In those positions the pin cannot yet be exploited. A smart exchange does the trick.

The positions without a pin are rather more difficult. Study them intently and be imaginative. If the positions prove to be too much to handle, then the trainer can give away the arrangement of the exercise sheet:
- 4x luring the front piece + pin
- 4x luring the front piece + attack on a pinned piece
- 4x luring the front piece + a pinned piece is not a good defender.

Mistake: The existing pin is incorrectly exploited.

Help: In position 2 1. Rae1 is rather tempting, but it runs into the sobering 1. … Qg2#. The same goes for position 8, where 1. Qc8 is met by 1. … Qh2#. Tell the students that they should check their answers.

Mistake: Position 5 is not solved correctly.

Help: The students have come as far as 1. Qf6+ Qg7, but the subsequent attack on the pinned queen with 2. Re7 is too difficult. Point out that the first move is correct.

□ *Pin / Placing front or back piece: A* ♖♖♖
Explanation: This page contains a mix of different themes.
Mistake: See the A- and B-pages.

□ *Pin / Placing the back piece: A*
1) 1. h6+ Kxh6 (1. ... Kg8 2. Qf6) 2. Qh1 (2. Rxd4 Kg7)
2) 1. e8Q+ Kxe8 2. Ba4; 1. Ba4? Rb1+
3) 1. Rh8+ Kxh8 2. Bc3; 1. ... Qxh8 2. Qg6#; 1. Bc3? Qxg3+ 2. fxg3 Bxh5 (often missed)
4) 1. g4+ Kxg4 2. Be6
5) 1. ... Nxd3 2. Qxd3 e5; 1. ... e5? 2. Bxc5

6) 1. Qxc6+ Rxc6 2. Nf4
7) 1. Nxc6 Qxc6 2. c4; 1. c4? Nde7
8) 1. ... Qf5 2. Bd3 d5
9) 1. Bh7+ Kxh7 2. Qxe6
10) 1. Bxc5 Qxc5 2. Qxd3; 1. Qxd3 cxd3 2. Bxc5, and 3. Bxc8 is nothing special.
11) 1. Nxc6 Qxc6 2. Qxc4
12) 1. Bxf7+! Kxf7 2. Qxe4; 1. Qxe4? Nxe4 2. Bxf7+ Kh8 (2. Rxf7 Nd6)

□ *Pin / Placing the front piece: A*
1) 1. Bxe5+ Nxe5 2. Qg3
2) 1. Rxf4+ Qxf4 2. Rf1
3) 1. Rxd6 Qxd6 2. Bg3
4) 1. e5 Qxe5 2. Re1
5) 1. Qf6+ Qg7 2. Re7! Qxf6 3. Rxh7#
6) 1. Rxe5 Rxe5 2. Re1
7) 1. Nxc5 Nxc5 2. Na4

8) 1. Rxc7+ Rxc7 2. Qc8
9) 1. ... Rxg2+ 2. Rxg2 Qxd2
10) 1. ... Qxf3+ (1. ... Ng4 2. hxg4) 2. Qxf3 Rxe2+
11) 1. Qxh7+ Qxh7 2. Nf7#; 1. Ng6+? Rxg6 2. Qxg6 Re1#
12) 1. e6 Bxe6 2. Qxg4

□ *Pin / Placing front or back piece: A*
1) 1. Bxd7+ Kxd7 2. Rh7
2) 1. ... Ra1+ Kxa1 2. Qxd2
3) 1. ... Rxf2+ 2. Kxf2 Bb6
4) 1. Qxc7 Rxc7 2. Bf4
5) 1. ... Qxg2+ 2. Qxg2 Rxf1+
6) 1. ... Rxc4+ 2. Bxc4 Qxe2
7) 1. ... Rxc3 2. Qxc3 Bf6

8) 1. ... Rxd4 2. Rxd4 c5
9) Drawing
10) 1. Qxd5+ Qxd5 2. Bg2; 1. Bg2 Bb7
11) 1. Rxb8 Kxb8 2. d4
12) 1. Qa3+ Re7 2. Ng8!

48

7   The passed pawn

AIM OF THE LESSON
- learning to use passed pawns
- learning to defend against passed pawns

PRIOR KNOWLEDGE
- all forms of eliminating the defender
- all forms of defence

ACQUISITION

Instruction
A pawn which can be advanced to the other side without encountering any of the opponent's pawns is called a passed pawn. The closer a passed pawn is to its promotion square, the more dangerous it is.

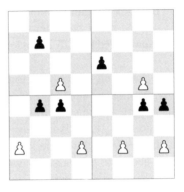

In the top left-hand part of the diagram (⇨) the c5-pawn is not a passed pawn, since the pawn on b7 controls the c6-square.
In the top right-hand part, the g5-pawn is a passed pawn. On the bottom left-hand part, Black can create a passed pawn by **1. ... b3** or **1. ... c3**. In the bottom right-hand part Black cannot create a passed pawn, since White controls the g3-square twice.

A passed pawn is a dangerous foe which must be stopped as early as possible. There are two ways to stop a passed pawn (diagram ⇩):
- blockading: occupying the square directly in front of the pawn.
- controlling: covering the square that the pawn can advance to. The pawn can still advance, but this, of course, is not wise.
There are a number of strategies available to

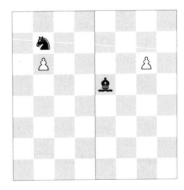

exploit a passed pawn. First, pieces can be used to help control the square directly in front of the passed pawn. The side with the passed pawn can also try to eliminate defenders with the help of combinations. For instance, the enemy piece that prevents pawn promotion can be eliminated through capturing, chasing away, blocking or interfering. This is therefore a suitable moment to refresh the students' knowledge of these types of combinations, which can be aimed specifically at helping passed pawns.

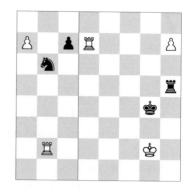

On the left part of the diagram (⇧) White plays **1. Rxb6** with the aim of promotion after **1. ... cxb6 2. a8Q**.

In the rook endgame on the right, White eliminates the black defender by means of an exchange: **1. Rd4+ Kf5 2. Rd5+**.

The diagram (⇨) contains four examples that involve chasing and luring away. In the top left-hand part, White's pawn is held under control by the king; 1. a7 is met by 1. ... Kb7. With **1. Bd5+** White lures the king away or denies him access to the passed pawn. Regardless of whether Black takes the bishop or plays **1. ... Kc7**, White pushes his pawn to a7 on the next move. In the top right-hand corner White wins material with **1. Bf7**. If Black takes the bishop, the pawn promotes; if Black does not take the bishop **2. g8Q** nets White a piece. In the bottom left-hand part Black lures the bishop on b2 away with **1. ... Ba3**.

In the bottom right-hand part, White can no longer stop the f-pawn after **1. ... Rh1+ 2. Kxh1 gxf2**.

In the next diagram (⇩) we consider two examples of interfering. On the left, the b-pawn marches on after **1. Rb6**, since **1. ... axb6** seals off the b-file.

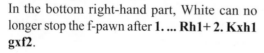

50

On the right, the h-pawn can still be held up by the bishop (1. ... h2 2. Be4). But this is no longer the case after **1. ... f3**. White's **2. exf3** closes off the long diagonal, after which the pawn is free to march on.

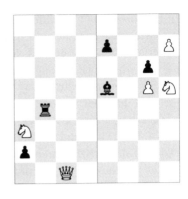

In the left part of the diagram (⇧) the white queen is covering a1 and b1, and the knight b1. With the interfering **1. ... Rb1** Black shuts off the queen. **2. Nxb1** is met by **2. ... a1Q**. On the right, the influence of the e5-bishop is eliminated in a similar fashion. After **1. Nf6** the h-pawn is unstoppable.

Promotion through blocking is the most beautiful method. In the diagram (⇨) White's h-pawn still has a long way to go. Black seems to have enough time to play d6 and ward off the pawn with his bishop. Black is in time after 1. h5 d6 2. Ke4 Kg3 3. h6 Kg4 and 4. ... Bf5+. White can win by blocking the d-pawn: **1. Bd6+ cxd6** (1. ... Kg2 2. h5 Bb7 3. h6 c5+ 4. Ke3) **2. h5** and the pawn marches through unhindered.

The next diagram (⇩) is for enthusiasts only. After 1. h7 a1Q+ 2. Qxa1 Rxa1+ Black can trade his rook against the last white pawn, after which White cannot win any more: 3. Kb7 Rb1+ 4. Kc7 Rc1+ 5. Kd7 Rd1+ 6. Ke7 Re1+ 7. Kf7 Rf1+ 8. Kg7 Rg1+ 9. Kh6 Rg2. White must gain time and prevent promotion of the black pawn first, even at the cost of a queen! With the beautiful **1. Qa1! Rxa1** the a-pawn is blocked. The win after **2. h7** is 'easy' (White has to win queen against rook and that requires some skill).

Finally, a promotion through a combination of luring and blocking. This example is rather difficult, but with proper explanation it can be made clear.

In the diagram (⇧) White must promote his h-pawn, otherwise he will have insufficient material to win. The direct 1. h7 runs into 1. ... e4, after which Black's king will reach the pawn. Hence, White must lure away the bishop from the long diagonal: **1. Ba7! Ba1** (1. ... Bxa7 2. h7) **2. Kb1** (otherwise 2. ... e4) **2. ... Bc3 3. Kc2 Ba1 4. Bd4!** (splendid move!) **4. ... Bxd4** (4. ... exd4 5. Kd3) **5. Kd3** (threatens 6. h7) **5. ... Ba1 6. Ke4** and the e-pawn is permanently blocked.

In students' games, the passed pawns of the opponent frequently advance unhindered. The second part of this lesson (which can be treated as a separate lesson) deals with ways of defending against passed pawns. Pawn promotion implies a material gain; promotion to a queen gives a player no fewer than eight points! The opponent must therefore aim to prevent promotion, even if this means the investment of material.

In the diagram (⇨) the knight must try to catch the a-pawn. The rook's pawn is the knight's bête noire. White can catch the pawn with **1. Nd3 a2 2. Nc1+**. Note that Black cannot make any progress with **1. ... Kc3 2. Nc1 Kc2 3. Na2**.

Bishops can generally deal with one passed pawn, but two passed pawns may be too much to handle. On the right, Black can no longer stop the pawn after 1. Be5? h4 2. Bf6 h3 3. Be5 d4. The correct move is **1. Bf2**. Both black pawns has to pass two dark squares. A pawn sacrifice doesn't work: **1. ... d4 2. Bxd4 h4 3. Be5**.

In some cases there is life after promotion, since the newly gained queen may be in jeopardy. In the diagram (⇩) Black cannot prevent c8Q. What he can do, however, is win the queen with **1. ... Ne5 2. c8Q Ng6+ 3. Kg8 Ne7+**. Note that 2. Kg8 Nc6 does not give White anything.

In the diagram (⇧) the promotion cannot be stopped, but the new queen can be won by **1. Nd2 c1Q 2. Rxb1+**. After **1. ... Nxd2 2. Rc1** and **3. Rxc2** Black does not retain sufficient material to win the game.

Escaping to a draw
Even when the passed pawn can no longer be stopped and the new queen cannot be won there may still be hope.
In the left part of the diagram (⇨) the black b-pawn is unstoppable. But White can reach a draw by stalemate. He draws immediately after **1. Ka3 b1Q** or **1. ... b1R**. White also gains half a point after **1. ... Nb1+ 2. Kb4** or **1. ... b1B 2. Kb4 Bd3 3. a4**, when the last pawn will disappear from the board.

On the right, White succeeds with **1. Rg4 h1Q** (after **1. ... h1R** White captures the bishop) **2. Rh4+ Qxh4**. It is stalemate.

Search strategy
We first consider the search strategy that deals with exploiting passed pawns. The students will have few problems finding a passed pawn. This leaves the question why that pawn cannot yet be promoted. That is, which defender must be eliminated, and how?
In the diagram (⇩) the passed pawn is in danger, since Black threatens 1. ... Kxf6, while 1. f7 is met by 1. ... Bd5+. White can lure the king away by playing **1. Bd4+ Kxd4** but then 2. f7 will still run into 2. ... Bd5+. White has no time for 2. Ba4 Bd5+ 3. Bb3 on account of 3. ... Ke5 4. f7 Bxf7. White must sacrifice his other bishop and get out of the check on d5: **2. Bc4 Kxc4 3. f7** with promotion.

In order to eliminate a passed pawn of the opponent an entirely different approach is called for. This can be done by capturing the pawn, winning the new queen or by stalemate. In the diagram (⇧) the pawn cannot be stopped. The king is guarding b1 and the pawn on e4 is guarding f3.

White has no time for Rb6-d6-d1 or Bh5-g6xe4. White can gain time by sacrificing a rook: **1. Rb1 Kxb1 2. Bg6 h1Q** (otherwise 3. Bxe4) **3. Bxe4+** and the new queen is lost by means of a double attack. The a-pawn will then decide matters.

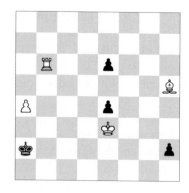

PRACTICE

Playing format

Bishop or knight against pawns
Stopping a pawn is an acquired art. Which of these pieces is better equipped to deal with pawns? The side with the pawn wins if the pawn reaches the other side of the board. After a few games the children will have found the right answer. The simultaneous display format is ideal for this game. The children can choose which side they want to play. The trainer can make the occasional mistake to test the children's skills. In both positions in the diagram (⇨) the pawn side wins with optimal play. This is also the case if, on the right, the knight side is to move first. It is not much fun playing the knight side. With reasonably correct play the pawns win without much effort.

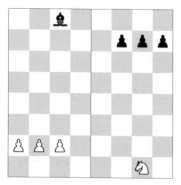

The side with the bishop is harder to beat. On the left, the pawn side can only win with **1. a4**. The bishop can be used more effectively when the pawns occupy more central positions. But even when the pawns are positioned on b2, c2 and d2 they prove to be unstoppable.

When the pawns are positioned closer to the centre still, as in the diagram (⇩), the road to victory is even smaller.

White to play, wins. If the bishop side is to play,
1. ... Bd7! is winning.

Workbook

☐ *Endgame / Passed pawn: A* ♖

Explanation: The aim is to exploit the passed pawn. The side with the passed pawn must win material, even if this means losing the passed pawn in the process. Some students think that the passed pawn must promote no matter what. This is not true; an exercise has been solved correctly when promotion of the passed pawn cannot be stopped anymore or when the side with the passed pawn has won material.

Mistake: The passed pawn does not lead to a material gain.

Help: Ask the students to indicate why the suggested answer is incorrect, and then ask them to look at the position again.

Mistake: The suggested answer for position 4 is 1. Rd6.

Help: 1. Rd6 wins material and is thus correct. Unfortunately, the move is insufficient for the win. Play out the position! (The students can also play against each other). The best course for Black is 1. ... g5 and then Kg8-g7-f7.

☐ *Endgame / Passed pawn: B* ♖ ♖

Explanation: See exercise sheet A.

Mistake: The passed pawn is played without due preparation (positions 1, 2, 10, 11 and 12).

Help: Execute the suggested move on the board and then ask the student to refute his own suggestion. The passed pawn can still be stopped. The defender must first be eliminated.

☐ *Endgame / Defending against the passed pawn: A* ♖

Explanation: The passed pawn of the opponent either has to be stopped or the new queen must be won. The passed pawn or new queen has to be eliminated at all cost, since allowing promotion would give the opponent eight extra points. An exercise has been solved correctly if the passed pawn no longer creates a danger.

Mistake: The passed pawn promotes anyway.

Help: Why is the answer wrong? Ask the student to look at the position once more.

Mistake: The piece stopping the passed pawn is positioned on the wrong

Help:

square (position 2: 1. ... Bg5 2. c7; position 3: 1. Be4 f5+).
The students have to find the right move themselves. If required,
they should spend more time on the positions.

ANSWERS

☐ *Endgame / Passed pawn: A*
1) 1. ... Bc1 2. Kh5 Bxf4; 2. ... g1Q?
   3. Nh3+
2) 1. ... Bb2
3) 1. ... e4+ 2. Bxe4 Nxe4
4) 1. Rxd8+ Nxd8 2. e7; 1. Rd6 g5 2.
   Rxc6 Kg7 is not sufficient.
5) 1. Rd7 Rxd7 2. exd7
6) 1. ... Be1+ 2. Ke2 b1Q 3. Rb5+

   Bb4; 2. Kxe1 b1Q+
7) 1. ... Qxf3 2. gxf3 e2
8) 1. Bh6+ Kxh7 2. Bxf8; 1. Bf6+?
   Kxh7
9) 1. Ne4; 1. Nf5? Re8
10) 1. Bc4+ Kh8 2. Bf7 or 2. Bb5
11) 1. Rxf8+ Kxf8 2. d7+
12) 1. ... Ra3 2. Rxa3 Bxd6+

☐ *Endgame / Passed pawn: B*
1) 1. Qc8+ Nxc8 2. d7
2) 1. Rh5 Rxh5 2. fxe7
3) 1. Qe6+ Qxe6 2. dxe6
4) 1. Rc7 d4 2. Rc8
5) 1. Nb7+ Nxb7 2. a6 Kc7 3. a7
6) 1. Be5+ Bxe5 (1. ... Kxe5 2. g7) 2.
   a7
7) 1. Rc8+ Rxc8 2. d7+; 1. d7+ Kf7

   2. Rc8 Ra5+
8) Drawing
9) 1. ... Qxc5 2. Nxc5 a7
10) 1. Rd8 Rxd8 2. Bf6+
11) Drawing
12) 1. Rg7+ Kh8 2. Rh7+ Kg8 3.
   Rh8+ Kxh8 4. g7+

☐ *Endgame / Defending against the passed pawn: A*
1) 1. Bb3 (1. Bb5? Kc2) 1. ... Kc1
   (1. ... Ka1 2. Bc2) 2. Ba2 ½-½
2) 1. ... b3+ 2. Kxb3 Ba5 ½-½
3) 1. Bd5+ Kg7 2. Ba2 ½-½
4) 1. Bc4+ Kxc4 2. Kxe2 Kc3 3. Kd1
   Kd3 stalemate
5) 1. Nd4 c1Q 2. Nf3#; 1. ... Kg5 2.
   Nxc2 1-0
6) 1. Bb1 (1. Bd3+? Kc3!) 1. ... Kb3
   (1. ... Kc3 2. Ba2) 2. Kd3 Kb2 3.

   Ba2 ½-½
7) 1. ... Nh1+ Kg2 2. Ke3 Kxh1 3.
   Kf2 stalemate
8) 1. ... Ke5 2. a7 Be6 3. a8Q Bd5+
   ½-½
9) 1. Bd7 Kxc7 2. Bxh3 ½-½
10) 1. Kf2 d1Q 2. Rxe1 1-0
11) 1. Kd7 a2 2. Ke7 a1Q 3. Bf6+
   ½-½
12) 1. Ne4 g2 2. Nd2+ ½-½

8   Eliminating the defence

AIM OF THE LESSON
• teaching tactical skills

PRIOR KNOWLEDGE
• all forms of eliminating the defence
• attack

ACQUISITION

Instruction
In lesson three about luring as a preparatory move we already outlined the importance of good prior knowledge. As we now discuss preparatory moves we are continuing from material which was discussed previously.

In this context 'eliminating the defender' is not an independent combination (as in Step 3), but rather a preparatory move that helps to set up a double attack.

Capturing
The easiest form of eliminating the defence is capturing. In the diagram (⇨) we see a double attack, only it does not work yet. The defender of the b6-square has to be captured in order to make the knight fork possible. White therefore plays **1. Bxd6 cxd6 2. Nc7+**, eliminating the defence by capturing in order to make a double attack possible.

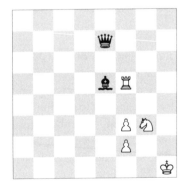

In the diagram (⇩) the rook on f5 is protected. It will soon become a victim of the double attack. First the defender of the target piece is taken: **1. ... Bxg3 2. fxg3** and after that the bounty is gathered with **2. ... Qh7+**. The preparatory capture is necessary, because if Black plays 1. ... Qh7+ straight away, White saves the rook by interposing the rook with 2. Rh5 when it is protected by the knight.

In the diagram (⇧) the same theme, eliminating by capturing, can be seen. Once again the bishop on c5 is the defender of b6. White first has to sacrifice his rook for the bishop in order to regain a rook. White wins material with **1. Rxc5 bxc5 2. Nb6+ Kb7 3. Nxa4.**
On the right, the queen on e1 is lost after **1. ... Rxg2+ 2. Kh1** (2. Rxg2 Nf3+) **2. ... Rh2+** (luring) **3. Kxh2 Nf3+.**
There is a difference between this and the previous two diagrams. In the first two there is an exchange, in the second one there is a sacrifice in order to eliminate the defender.

Chasing and luring away
On the left in the diagram (⇨) White plays **1. d4** in order to chase the rook away from c5. After **1. ... Rc6 2. Qa5+** follows with the win of a bishop. The defender is eliminated by chasing away in order to make a double attack with the queen possible.

On the right, the defender has to be lured away. It is clear that a knight fork wins the queen. Have the students find out which of the two knight moves leads to the desired goal. Winning is **1. ... Nh3+ 2. gxh3 Nf3+.** After another knight move Black wins nothing: 1. ... Nf3+ 2. gxf3 Nh3+ 3. Bxh3.

Interfering
Interfering can obviously also be used as a preparatory move.
In the diagram (⇩) giving check with 1. Qd6+ does not amount to anything because both rooks are protected. With the surprising **1. Nb5** the connection between the two rooks is broken, after which a double attack on c7 or d6 becomes possible, all depending on which move Black

will play.

Also on the right, Black wins material by interfering. After **1. ... g4** it is best for White to give up the knight or the bishop or else a knight fork on f3 will follow.

X-ray

Also preparation is sometimes needed for an X-ray check.

On the left in the diagram (⇧) 1. ... Ra2+ 2. Ba3 Nb6+ 3. Kb3 surprisingly loses an exchange. Black can eliminate White's defence with **1. ... Nb6+ 2. Bxb6 Ra2+** and that wins an exchange. On the right, White seems to win a rook with 1. Rhg4+ but this is not true. After 1. ... Kh6 the black rooks protect each other and the win is gone. The preparatory move is really necessary. First of all the rook on g1 has to be chased away with **1. Kh2**. Then after **1. ... Ra1 2. Rhg4+** White wins a rook.

Blocking

Even blocking as a preparatory move is seen sometimes, often in combination with 'chasing' (see lesson 12). In the diagram (⇨) the X-ray check 1. Rd8+ does not win any material after 1. ... Ke4. White therefore has to make the king move impossible with the blocking move **1. e4+ Rxe4** (or 1. ... Kd6 2. Rd8+) **2. Rd8+** and now White does win the rook.

In-between check

The defence against the X-ray attack in the diagram (⇩) consists of avoiding a saving check. The direct 1. Rg2 will lose the rook after 1. ... Ne3+. Also after 1. Re1+ Kc2 2. Rg1 Black saves himself with a check on e3. First moving the king out of reach of a check is the correct way to win material. White can threaten mate on e1 with **1. Kb3**. After **1. ... Kc1 2. Rg2** is winning.

Search strategy

The search strategy is not difficult with this preparatory move. There is a double attack in the position, which does not work yet because there is a defence. The defender which is preventing this double attack, has to be eliminated. In the diagram (⇑) White still has sufficient control over the e4 pawn, losing a defender will be fatal. With **1. ... Bb4** Black attacks a defender with tempo. White first has to defend his knight. After **2. Bd2 Bxc3 3. Bxc3 dxe4** White loses a piece.

Reminder
◊ *Double attack: elimination of the defence*

Workbook

☐ *Double attack / Eliminating the defence: A* ♖

Explanation: A double attack on the knight is not possible yet. With the known means of eliminating the defence (capturing, chasing away, luring away and interfering - blocking does not show up here) a double attack can be made to work.

Mistake: The solution is wrong.

Help: "Which pieces are a knight's move away?" and "Which of these prevents the knight fork?"

Mistake: Position 5 is wrong.

Help: The knight fork makes use of the pin on the c-file. In the initial position there are still two pieces on the c-file, which is why it is difficult to see the target.

☐ *Double attack / Eliminating the defence: B* ♖

Explanation: A double attack of the queen does not work yet. There can be many different reasons for that;
  • A target is still protected.
  • The opponent's piece is in the way. The square for the queen is still in enemy hands.
  • The solution is obvious: the defender has to be eliminated.

Mistake:	The solution is wrong.
Help:	With questions like "Which target you see?", "Do you see a second target?" Or "Where would the queen love to give check?" every student will come to the correct answer.

☐ *Double attack / Eliminating the defence: A*
1) 1. Bxc6+ Bxc6 2. Ne5+ (capturing)
2) 1. Qxe5 Rxe5 2. Nf6+ (capturing)
3) 1. a5 Nc8 2. Nd5 (chasing away)
4) 1. Qxe8+ Rxe8 2. Nc6+ (capturing)
5) 1. ... d4 2. Ne4 Nb3+ (chasing away)
6) 1. ... Qxf3 2. gxf3 Ne2+ (capturing)
7) 1. Bxc7 winning a pawn (luring away)
8) 1. ... Bxb2 (capturing)
9) 1. Rxf7+ Rxf7 2. Ne6+ (capturing)
10) 1. Bxb7 Bxb7? 2. Ne6+ (luring away)
11) 1. ... Nhxf3+ 2. Bxf3 Nxh3+ (luring away)
12) 1. ... g4 2. Nf4 Nf3+ (interfering)

☐ *Double attack / Eliminating the defence: B*
1) 1. d5 Ne5 2. Qa4+ (chasing away)
2) 1. Bxc6 dxc6 2. Qa3+ (capturing)
3) 1. Nxf5 exf5 2. Qxd5+ (luring away)
4) 1. f4 Re7 2. Qb2+; 1. Qb2? Qb6+ (chasing away)
5) 1. Ng5 fxg5 2. Qh5+; 1. ... g6 2. Qh4+ (interfering)
6) 1. Bxf6 Qxf6 2. Qd5+ (capturing)
7) 1. Nxg6+ hxg6 2. Qh4+ (luring away)
8) 1. ... Ne3 2. fxe3 Qxe3+ (luring)
9) 1. Re7 Qxe7 2. Qxd5+ (luring away)
10) 1. ... Bxg2 2. Qxg2 Qa5 (luring away)
11) 1. Nd4 exd4 2. Qb3+ (interfering)
12) 1. ... a6 (or first 1. ... Qg6+ and 2. ... a6) 2. Qb3 Qg6+ (chasing away)

9   The magnet

- learning a new attacking technique
- the importance of a gain of tempo

PRIOR KNOWLEDGE
- mating patterns

ACQUISITION

Instruction
Up to this point we have covered a number of different types of combinations that are aimed at a direct attack on the king. These comprise the different forms of eliminating the defender and the mate in two exercises.
In this lesson we will discuss the final form of a combination aimed at the enemy king.
Sometimes, even though you have sufficient material, the enemy king can still escape a mating attack.

The magnet
In the diagram (⇨) Black meets the obvious
1. Qh7+ by 1. ... Kf8, after which the king can escape via e7. White must try to keep the enemy king on the kingside. This can be achieved with
1. Rh8+, which forces the king to h8. After **1. ... Kxh8 2. Qh7** Black is mated. This type of combination is called a **magnet**, a term that speaks for itself.
In the left part of the diagram (⇩), 1. Qa4 is met by 1. ... cxb6. Instead **1. Ra8+** is called for: **1. ... Kxa8 2. Qa4+ Kb8 3. Qa7#**.
On the right, the students have to imagine that White has a forced mate somewhere on the board. This can best be done by putting the

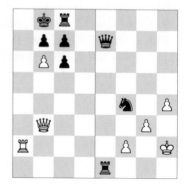

position on a demonstration board. What Black must do is work with a gain of tempo, which is the essence of the magnet. Black can do this by **1. ... Rh1+ 2. Kxh1 Qe1+ 3. Kh2 Qxf2+ 4. Kh1 Qg2#.**
This gain of tempo is of the utmost importance. The piece that has to deliver the mate must be put in position with the help of a check.

We can stress the importance of the tempo by using the upper part of the diagram (⇑). The standard attack 1. Qd8+ Kh7 2. Qf8 is too slow. Black has enough time to defend or even organise his own attack. After **1. Qf8+ Kxf8 2. Rd8#**, however, White wins.
In the lower part of the diagram Black is faced with a mating threat, and so he has no time for 1. ... Nc3. Rather, the knight has to move with tempo (i.e. with check) to c3: **1. ... Ra2+ 2. Kxa2 Nc3+ 3. Ka1 Rb1#.**
In the left part of the diagram (⇒) Black can home in with **1. ... Ra2+** (but not 1. ... Qa5, when the king escapes to c1) **2. Kxa2 Qa5+ 3. Kb2 Qa3#.** If White does not take on a2 he will be mated on c2.

On the right, we see an example of how the king can be lured in front of his protective cover of pawns. After **1. g6+ Kxg6** (or 1. ... Kg8 2. Qf7+) **2. Qf5#** Black is mated.

Combining motives
The magnet combination is often used alongside other combinatory motifs. In the left part of the diagram (⇓) the magnet goes hand in hand with a pin. White forces the king to a8 with the help of a rook sacrifice, thereby pinning the b-pawn: **1. Ra8+ Kxa8 2. Qxa6+ Kb8 3. Qxb7#.**
On the right, we see an example of the same type of combination, but with a twist. The knight is not a good defender of h1, since it is pinned. Black wins with **1. ... Rh1+ 2. Kxh1** (2. Nxh1 Qxg2#) **2. ... Qh3+ 3. Kg1 Qxg2#.**

The diagram (⇧) contains two rather more difficult examples. On the left, Black is threatening 1. ... Ra1+ 2. Kb4 Ra4. White has no time to get a new queen, but he does have a solution to his predicament: **1. Bb6+ Kxb6** (after 1. ... Ka8 White queens) **2. c8N+! Ka5 3. b4#.**

On the right, we can see an example of a characteristic attacking position. After the direct 1. Qh4 Black defends with 1. ... Re8, when 2. Qh7+ Kf8 does not give White anything. Another problem for White is the bishop on g7, which prevents 3. Qxf7#. With **1. Rh8+** White kills two birds with one stone. **1. ... Kxh8** obviously runs into **2. Qh4+** and **3. Qh7#** while **1. ... Bxh8** is met by **2. Qh4 Re8 3. Qh7+ Kf8 4. Qxf7#** or **4. Qxh8#.**

At Step 4 level, students will appreciate the beauty of the magnet in the diagram (⇨), in particular if they have searched in vain for a solution. White's only road to victory is **1. Qa4+ Kxa4 2. Ra1+** (this move had to be with a gain of tempo) **2. ... Kb5 3. Bd7#.**

Search strategy

The magnet combination itself is not that difficult. All it takes is a basic knowledge of mating patterns. Having found a suitable mating pattern, the students should go on to find a sacrifice; this makes it possible for an attacking piece to give check with a gain of tempo.

In the diagram (⇩) White's problem is that the e1-rook cannot take part in the action. Otherwise, 1. Qg8+ or 1. Qh5+ would win easily. The only mating pattern that White can aim for involves the queen on e8. This can be achieved with the help of a magnet: **1. Rf8+ Kxf8 2. Qh8+ Kf7 3. Qe8+.**

As can be seen, the e1-rook takes part in the action after all. The solution is easy, but most students will nevertheless find this position difficult.

Workbook

☐ *Mate / Magnet: A*   ♖

Explanation: The magnet sacrifice gives the attacker time to bring out his most important attacking pieces with tempo. With the help of a sacrifice, the enemy king is drawn into a mating net (mate in two, three or four moves).

Mistake: The king can escape.

Help: This means that there was probably no magnet sacrifice. Looking at the position once more is usually sufficient.

☐ *Mate / Magnet: B*   ♖ ♖

Explanation: See exercise sheet A.

Mistake: The suggested solution to position 1 is 1. Rc1+ Kd6 2. Qd8#.

Help: Look at the queen on b5 and the king on f1. White is in check! Try again.

ANSWERS

☐ *Mate / Magnet: A*

1) 1. Re8+ Kxe8 2. Qe7#
2) 1. Rh8+ Kxh8 2. Qh7#
3) 1. Qh6+ Kxh6 2. Rh1#; 1. ... Kg8 2. Rc8+ and mate
4) 1. ... Ra3+ 2. Kxa3 Qa6 and mate
5) Drawing
6) Drawing
7) 1. a4+ Kxa4 2. Qb3+

8) 1. Qf8+ Kxf8 2. Rxf7+ Ke8 3. Rf8+ Kd7 4. R2f7#
9) 1. Rh8+ Kxh8 2. Qe8+ Kh7 3. Qg8#
10) 1. Rh8+ Qxh8 2. Qf7#
11) 1. ... Rh2+ 2. Kxh2 Qf4+ 3. Kh1 Qf3+ 4. Kh2 Qg2#
12) 1. Qf6+ Kxf6 2. Be5#; 1. ... Kg8 2. Be5 with mate.

☐ *Mate / Magnet: B*

1) 1. Rc4+ Kxc4 2. Qc3#
2) 1. Rxh7+ Kxh7 2. Qf7+ Kh6 3. Qxg6#; 2. ... Kh8 3. Nxg6#
3) 1. ... Qh1+ 2. Kxh1 Bf3+ 3. Kg1 Rd1#
4) 1. Qf8+ Kxf8 2. Rd8#
5) 1. ... Bd3+ 2. Kxd3 Qd1#
6) 1. ... Qg1+ 2. Kxg1 Rbxg2+ 3. Kh1 Rg1+ 4. Rxg1 Nf2#; 2. Rxg1 Nf2#

7) 1. Rb8+ Kxb8 2. Rh8#
8) 1. ... Rh1+ 2. Kxh1 Qh3+ 3. Kg1 Nf3#
9) 1. ... Rg1+ 2. Kxg1 Qxh2+ 3. Kf1 Qh1#
10) 1. ... Ra3+ 2. Kxa3 Qa1+ 3. Kb3 a4#
11) 1. ... Bxh3 2. Kxh3 Qf4 and mate on g3.
12) 1. Rh7+ Kxh7 2. Qh2+

10   Weak pawns

AIM OF THE LESSON
• learning (some) basic positional skills

PRIOR KNOWLEDGE
• attacking targets
• piece activity

ACQUISITION

Instruction
For beginners positional aspects are much more difficult to comprehend than tactical ones. This should come as no surprise, since combinations and other tactical motifs have a direct result, whereas positional moves do not. For this reason, we will restrict our attention to positional aspects that involve 'visual' factors.

Weak pawns are easy to spot. A pawn is weak when:
• it cannot be protected by another pawn.
• it is an easy target for attack.

In the diagram (⇩) the pawn on f6 is weak on both counts. The pawns on f7 and h7 are also weak but less so, because they cannot be easily attacked. We might therefore say that f7 and h7 are semi-weak.

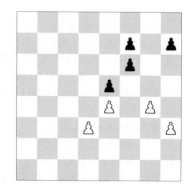

The pawn on d3 is very weak (on both counts) and the pawn on h3 is semi-weak, because the latter cannot be attacked so easily.
While these characteristics can be seen straight from the position, it is always important to take into account the remaining pieces. If a black rook could enter on the second rank and go to h2 matters would be different.

In the diagram (⇧) the white pawn on h2 is weak. We can eliminate this weakness by advancing it to h4, but then the pawn on g3 will become weak, and all we have done is replace one problem with another. Black has a weak pawn on c7. By playing this pawn to c5, both b6 and d6 will become weak. In other words, advancing the c-pawn doubles Black's problems. Most of the time pawns such as those on h3 and c7 are best left standing, since advancing them creates other, more serious problems.

Weak pawns are weak only to the extent that the weaknesses can be exploited. The crucial question is whether the opponent can attack them. If the opponent lacks the right pieces for this, the weakness is not much of a problem. If there are as many attackers as defenders, weaknesses can pose a problem. A piece that has to defend a weak pawn loses its mobility and is vulnerable, given that it is tied to a particular spot.

In pawn endings, weak pawns, and especially doubled pawns, are particularly vulnerable. In pawn endings the only defender is the king, and his task involves much more than defending alone.

It is instructive to play the position in the diagram (⇨) to a finish. The students can play against each other or simultaneous against the trainer. With correct play Black wins, although he requires a healthy dose of endgame technique for this. The first move can be taken as an indicator of the student's strength. It is an advantage to move first.

The pawn structure on the queenside is the same in the following diagram (⇩), but the overall position is of a quite different nature. Here White's piece activity more than compensates for the weak pawns on the c-file. The bishop on a3 prevents Black from castling. As a result, Black cannot bring his king to safety and he is prevented from bringing out his rook.

An extensive discussion is instructive. One variation is **1. 0-0-0 Bxc3 2. Rd3 Ba5 3. Rhd1 f6 4. Rd7 b5 5. Re7+ Kf8 6. Rdd7**.

The diagram (⇧) offers another illustration of the need to take into account more than the pawn structure alone. It turns out that White's pawns are not weak at all: **1. Nf3 Bc6 2. Kd4 Bd7 3. Ne5 Be8 4. Nd3 Bd7 5. Nc5 Bc8 6. b3 Be6 7. Nxa6 Bg8 8. Nc5 Bf7 9. Nd3 Be8 10. Nf4 Bf7 11. g3** and White wins.

It is important to emphasise that doubled pawns are not always weak. At Step 4 level students tend to jump at the opportunity to give their opponent doubled pawns, even when this means giving up an active piece.

There is a direct link between **weak** pawns and strong squares. Using the diagram (⇨) we outline the characteristics of a **strong** square:

- a strong square cannot be controlled by the opponent's pawns.
- a strong square is available to one of your own pieces.
- a strong square is protected by one of your own pawns.
- a strong square is located in or around the part of the board where the main action takes place (this is usually the centre of the board).

In the diagram the squares b5 and d5 are strong squares for White; f5 is not a strong square, since Black can control it by playing g6. Black has strong squares on d4 and f4. The c5 square is not strong because White's b-pawn can still exert an influence on it. An important factor, of course, is that the knight can leap to a strong square via e2 and c3; the same goes for the black knight, which can reach a strong square via e6. The squares f5 and f6 are a different story. Ideally, the g7-pawn must cover both squares, but in reality it can cover only one. This means that one of the two squares will always be strong for White. It is up to Black to decide which square this will be. A strong square, once under control, must be very well protected.

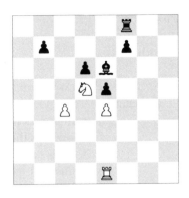

In the diagram (⇧) White's knight is placed on the strong square d5, but it is attacked by the bishop. If White leaves the knight where it is Black would exchange it, after which the square will be occupied by a pawn and will no longer be strong. A further drawback of this exchange is that it promotes the pawn on d6 from weak to semi-weak, since this pawn is now no longer vulnerable. White has two ways to avoid the exchange. One is to move away the knight, and move it back when Black no longer controls d5. The other is to support the knight by another knight, so that after an exchange a new knight will appear on the strong square.

A good understanding of weak pawns and strong squares does not come easily. It is important to focus on these two aspects when discussing student's games.

Search strategy
We outline the right approach to solving the exercise sheet 'Pawn structure' with the help of the diagram (⇩). The first point to note is that Black's king is better placed than its white counterpart, although this advantage is only temporary (the white king is better off on g1). In addition, Black's pieces are also more active than White's (e.g. the bishop). Both sides have a set of doubled pawns. Black can remove this weakness by **1. ... Qf5+**. After **2. Qxf5 gxf5** he has improved both his pawn structure and the activity of his bishop, which now ties the white rook to the protection of the c3-pawn.

Workbook

☐ *Strategy / Pawn structure: A*   ♖

Explanation: The students must indicate the move which:
- improves their own pawn structure
- worsens the opponent's pawn structure
- leads to an important increase of piece activity (even when this is at the cost of a weakened pawn structure)
- prevents the opponent from improving his pawn structure.

              Point out that the gain will be modest (as compared to the exercises that they are accustomed to).

Mistake: The suggested solution is wrong.

Help: Using direct questions we can ascertain whether the goal is to inflict damage on the opponent or to improve one's own position. If this fails, then a step-by-step approach is in order, with the kind of questions depending on the exercise: "Can you burden your opponent with a doubled pawn?" or "Can you loosen the opponent's pawns?"

Help: Play the position to a finish. All positions are suitable.

☐ *Test / Mix: E*   ♖

Explanation: The themes of the exercises have been taken from previous lessons (placing the front piece and back piece, exploiting a passed pawn, double attack, eliminating the defender, magnet). Remind the students of the topics concerned.

Mistake: The suggested answer is wrong.

Help: Turn to the relevant section in the workbook and direct the student's attention to a similar exercise. "How did you solve this exercise?"

Mistake: (Too) many mistakes.

Help: What is the cause of these mistakes? If the mistakes are caused by a lack of knowledge, then it is advisable to go over the material once more.

☐ *Test / Mix: F*   ♖ ♖

Explanation: The themes of the exercises have been taken from both this and previous Steps.

☐ *Strategy / Pawn structure: A*

1) **1. ... c5 2. bxc5 Bxc5**
The black bishop has become more active; in addition, White's pawn structure has been weakened.

2) **1. Nd5+ and 2. Nxf6**
The black pawn structure has been weakened; the pawn on f7 is particularly weak. Black can try to play f5 and f6, but then f5 will become a target for the white bishop.

3) Drawing

4) **1. ... g5 2. fxg6? Bxg4**
The pin against the white f-pawn gives Black the opportunity to remove his backward pawn. The rook is no longer tied to the protection of the h-pawn.

5) **1. Bxc6+ bxc6 2. Qxf3**
Before taking back on f3, White first weakens the opponent's pawn structure.

6) Drawing

7) **1. f5 Bxc4 2. bxc4**
White accepts doubled pawns. Black cannot protect his weak pawn anymore. Black has nothing to worry about after 1. Bxe6 fxe6.

8) **1. e5 Bc7 2. Bxg6**
White does not take on d5 because after 1. exd5 exd5 leaves him with a weak and extremely vulnerable pawn on e3. For this reason, White prefers to advance his e-pawn with tempo, thereby giving Black weak doubled g-pawns.

9) **1. Rc1 c5 2. Rc4**
It goes without saying that White does not exchange on d5. The weak pawn on c6 must remain on the board. The rook is the best piece to attack the weak c- and a-pawns.

10) **1. ... h4 2. Bxe5 dxe5**
Black gets a strong pawn duo in the centre.

11) **1. h5 Bf5 2. h6**
Advancing the h-pawn worsens the black pawn structure after 2. ... gxh6 3. Bxf6 or 2. ... Bf8, when it is up to White to determine when to take on g7.

12) **1. Re2**
It would be foolish to exchange the weak pawn on e5 for the pawn on f2. White can still take the pawn on the next move.

□ *Test / Mix: E*

1) 1. Bc3 Bxc3 2. c7; 1. c7? Bxc7 2. Bxc7 Kg5 (exploiting a passed pawn)
2) 1. ... Rxd4 2. Rxd4 Qg5 or 1. ... Qg5 (double attack: eliminating the defender)
3) 1. Nxd5, winning a pawn (placing the front piece)
4) 1. ... Rg1+ 2. Kxg1 Nf3+ 3. Kh1 Qh2# (magnet)
5) 1. d6 Bxd6 2. Rb6 (placing the front piece)
6) 1. Rh8+ Kxh8 2. Qxh6+ Kg8 3. Qxg7# (placing the back piece)
7) 1. Nd8 or 1. Bd8 (interfering)
8) 1. Ke3 Ng5 2. Bf6+; 1. ... Nd6 2. Bc5 (exploiting a passed pawn)
9) 1. ... Qxf3+ 2. Kxf3 Nh4+ 3. Kf4 g5# (mate)
10) 1. ... Rxc1 2. Rxc1 Qh6 (double attack: luring)
11) 1. Nc6! Rxe3 2. Qxc2; 1. ... Rxc6 2. Rxe7 (interfering)
12) 1. ... Qxe2 2. Rxe2 f6 (placing the back piece)

□ *Test / Mix: F*

1) 1. ... Bxe3 2. fxe3 Nc2 (double attack: luring)
2) 1. f4 Bd6 2. Qxe6+ (attacking a pinned piece)
3) 1. Qa8 Rxa8 2. Nxe7+ (double attack: eliminating the defender)
4) 1. Qf8+ Kxf8 2. Rh8#; 1. ... Rxf8 2. Ne7# (luring away + mate / blocking)
5) 1. ... Be7 2. Qxg5 Bxg5+; 2. Rdh1 Qxf4 3. Rxf4 Bg5 (double attack)
6) 1. ... Be2 2. f3 Nxg3; 2. Qxe2 hxg6 (defending against a pin)
7) 1. Bc4 Rg7 2. Rh8+ (double attack: eliminating)
8/9) Drawing
10) 1. Rh7+ Rxh7 2. Qxg5+ Kxg5 3. d8Q+ (passed pawn)
11) 1. ... Bf6+ 2. Bc3 Qd2 (placing the front piece)
12) 1. Qg8+ Kxg8 2. Ng6 (mate)

11   Material advantage

AIM OF THE LESSON
- learning endgame tactics
- learning to convert a material advantage in the endgame.

PRIOR KNOWLEDGE
- key squares

ACQUISITION

Instruction
In this lesson we consider what it takes to win an endgame when you are a pawn up, taking rook endgames as our point of departure. A number of general rules will be formulated. These are to some extent also applicable to other types of endgames.

Cutting off
In the diagram (⇨) White is two pawns up. Both sides have a king and a rook. White must try to keep the king and the rook away from his pawns, and bring his own pieces into play at the same time. In this position the black king is unable to take part, since the white rook is restricting it to the other side of the board. In such cases, we say that the rook is 'cutting off' the king. To win, White's king first has to head towards its pawns. It is essential that this is done before the pawns are advanced. Black can defend with his rook only. We play: **1. Kd2 Re7** (Black tries to keep the king away) **2. Re3** (White does not have to cut off the king anymore, since the pawn ending is easily won) **2. ... Rf7 3. Ke2** (the king moves towards the pawns) 3. ... Kd7 **4. Kf3** (diagram ⇩). Now that the white pieces have been brought into position, the pawns are

ready to advance.

It is instructive to play this position to a finish using a simultaneous display format. The students play with the white pieces and must try to win. Most of them will succeed. They are allowed to take back a move if they blunder. The most important endgame goals are:

1) a pawn advance must be supported by its own pieces.
2) defenders must be eliminated (by cutting them off or by exchanging them).

In the case at hand, the endgame is won by cutting off the enemy king and by offering an exchange of rooks.

It is a good idea to discuss some additional examples on the demonstration board. In each of these the students must try to find the best move.

In the diagram (⇨) White's best option is to play **1. Rd2**, cutting off the enemy king. The general rule regarding this is as follows: the further away (i.e. the more files) the king is cut off, the better.

Building a bridge

In the diagram (⇩) the white pawns are far removed from their own pieces. White must first bring his king towards the pawns. This can only be achieved by chasing away the enemy rook with **1. Re3**. After 1. ... **Rd7** White 'steals' another file by playing **2. Ke2** and **3. Rd3**. Assisting the king in this way is appropriately called 'building a bridge'.

Building a bridge is successful only when, in the event of a rook exchange, the ensuing pawn ending is won. In the present example, where White is two pawns up, White can safely transpose to a pawn ending. In other case, the side that is building a bridge can even offer a pawn in the process.

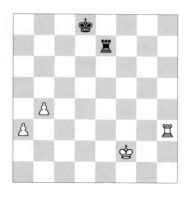

Transposing to a won ending
In the diagram (⇧) White can opt for the 'safe' approach with **1. Kd2**, in which case he must still work hard to bring home the point. However, armed with the knowledge of key squares (as outlined in Step 3), White can also transpose to a pawn ending with **1. Rc5+**. This move loses a pawn, but after the exchange of rooks a familiar position has arisen: **1. ... Rxc5 2. bxc5 Kc6 3. Kd3 Kxc5** (3. ... Kd5 4. c6!) **4. Kc3** and Black cannot prevent the white king from reaching one of the key squares (i.e. b4, c4 or d4).

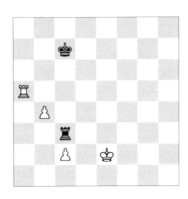

The side with the pawn up must be careful to transpose to a pawn ending, since this is not always sufficient to win. In the left part of the diagram (⇨) Black can draw with **1. ... Rxb4+**, since White is unable to win the pawn ending that arises after **2. Kxb4 Kxc6**. Put the position on a demonstration board and ask one of the students to hold the draw, just to make sure. On the right, the quickest road to victory is **1. Re7+!** After **1. ... Rxe7 2. f6+ Kf7 3. fxe7 Kxe7 4. Kh5! Kf7 5. Kh6 Kg8 6. Kg6** the pawn can no longer be stopped.

Winning a position of the kind as shown in the diagram (⇩) is more difficult. Black still has a pawn, and so White will have to create a passed pawn to win. However, the general rules introduced above still hold: bring your own pieces into play first, and restrict your opponent's pieces as much as possible.
A possible course of the game is: **1. Rd2** (cutting off the king) **1. ... Re8 2. Re2** (offering an exchange and building a bridge for the king) **2. ... Rd8+ 3. Ke1 Rd7 4. Kf2 Kd8**.
Now the time is ripe to create a passed pawn: **5. h4 Rf7 6. Kf3** (not 6. h5? Rf5) **6. ... Kd7 7. h5 Kd8 8. Kg4 Kd7 9. Kg5 Kd8 10. h6**. White cleverly exchanges the rook pawn. This allows him to retain connected pawns without having a pawn on the edge of the board.

The diagram (⇧) contains a position which the students, as White, can play to a finish. White has to tread carefully, since Black's pieces have not been cut off and so can take part in the defence. For those students who show good endgame technique the position can be made more difficult by moving all pieces one file to the right. The ending with the pawns on the g- and h-file is harder, since the edge of the board is in the way. A further complication is that once the pawns reach the 6th and 7th ranks, White has to watch out for stalemate.

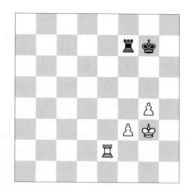

It is a good idea to also play these positions to a finish, once again using a simultaneous format. It is not advisable to ask the students to play these positions against each other. In such positions young, inexperienced players usually do not choose the best defence.

Students who finish their games quickly can go on to do the exercise sheet on passed pawns in rook endgames. These puzzles test the general ability how to cash in a passed pawn in these endings.

The diagram (⇨) contains an example. It would be too simple to play 1. b7 Rxc7+ and White loses. Since Black's king is nearby, exchanging rooks is a real threat.
White uses a technique worthwhile to recall: **1. Ra7!** This move avoids the exchange of rooks, the a-pawn would be unstoppable. Now 2. b7 is a threat impossible to prevent: **1. ... Kd6** (1. ... Kd8 2. b7 is the same) **2. b7 Kc7** (2. ... Rd8 3. Ra8) **3. b8Q+ Kxb8 4. Rxd7.**

Workbook

☐ *Rook ending / Passed pawn: A* ♖

Explanation: The side that is to move can use his passed pawn to obtain a material gain. This does not necessarily involve a pawn promotion; the exercise has also been solved correctly when the opponent is forced to give up material. The main weapon is that of eliminating the defender, primarily by means of luring away and interfering. In many positions a useful ploy is to build a bridge by placing a rook between an attacking piece and the passed pawn. Another use for the rook is to take control of the promotion square.

Mistake: The correct solution is not found.

Help: "Why is the passed pawn unable to advance? Eliminate the defender or mobilise your own pieces" (depending on the exercise concerned).

Mistake: The suggested answer to assignment 10 is 1. Rc5+.

Help: The student is content with luring away the rook, which was also the correct strategy in position 2. Make sure that the student discovers the mistake himself. Finding the right move will then no longer be a problem.

ANSWERS

☐ *Rook ending / Passed pawn: A*

1) 1. Ra6 Rxa6 2. bxa6 and 3. a8Q+
2) 1. Rd6+ Rxd6 2. b8Q
3) 1. Rh3+ Kg8 2. Rg3 Rxg3 3. d7; 1. Rf8+? Kh7 2. Rd8 Rg5 3. Kd2 Kg7
4) 1. ... Rg4+ 2. Kc5 Rh4 with promotion.
5) 1. Re3 Kxe3 2. e7 Rd1+ 3. Kc2 Rd2+ 4. Kc1 with promotion
6) 1. Rd4 Kxd4 2. d7 with promotion.
7) 1. ... Rd1+ 2. Kxd1 exf2 and Black promotes.
8) 1. h6+ Kg8 2. h7+ Kg7 3. Rxf8
9) 1. ... Rb2+ 2. Ke3 Rb3+ 3. Rxb3 a1Q or 2. Kd1 Rb1+
10) 1. Kb4 Ra1 2. Rc5+ and 3. Ra5; 1. Rc5+?? Rxc5 with check!
11) 1. exd6 Rxe1+ 2. Kf2 Re8 3. dxc7 and 4. d6
12) 1. ... Rc1! followed by 2. ... d2 because 2. Ke3 is met by 2. ... Re1+

12 Chasing and targeting

AIM OF THE LESSON
• extending the level of tactical skills

PRIOR KNOWLEDGE
• preparatory moves
• double attack

ACQUISITION

Instruction
We begin this lesson by repeating the types of preparatory moves that involve luring and eliminating the defence. These were introduced in the preceding lessons 3 and 8. The present lesson introduces two new types of preparatory moves: **chasing** and **targeting** (aiming).

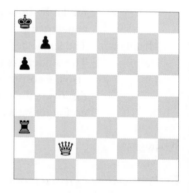

Chasing
We use the term 'chasing' when a king or another piece is forced to a square on which it is subsequently subject to a double attack.

In the diagram (⇨) White does not yet have a double attack available. However, the rook on a3 is unprotected and White can give a check. With **1. Qc8+** the king is chased to a7, thereby permitting the double attack **2. Qc5+**. White wins a rook.

In the diagram (⇩) White can win the queen with an X-ray check. For this the black king has to be chased to the a2/g8 diagonal or the g-file first. White wins with **1. Qd4+ Kf5** (1. ... Ke6 2. Qc4+) **2. Qe4+!** (Careful, a wrong check leads nowhere: 2. Qf4+? Kg6 3. Qg4+ Kf7) **2. ... Kg5 3. Qg2+**.

Chasing is also possible with other pieces, of course.

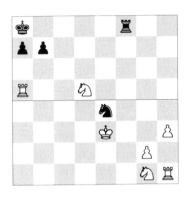

In the upper part of the diagram (⇧) White plays **1. Nb6+**, making use of the pinned a-pawn. After the forced **1. ... Kb8 2. Nd7+** brings in the loot.

We can chase other pieces than the king. In the lower part of the diagram Black first chases the rook to h2 with **1. ... Ng3**, and then picks it up with **2. ... Nf1+**.

In the left part of the diagram (⇨) the knight fork is still a long way away. The contours of the fork emerge after **1. b3+ Ka5 2. b4+**. The king must step into the knight's range, given that the alternative is **2. ... Ka4 3. Nc3#** is not attractive. After both **2. ... Kb5** and **2. ... Ka6** the knight check on c7 decides.

On the right, Black is in dire straits after **1. Nf5+**. The f-file is a no-go area on account of the discovered check **2. Nh6+**, while **1. ... Kg6** is met by **2. Ne7+**. Going to the h-file takes one move longer: **1. ... Kh7** (1. ... Kh8 2. Rh3#) **2. Rh3+ Kg6 3. Ne7+**.

In the diagram (⇩) White is a lot of material behind, but his rampant knight more than makes up for this. The win of the queen is obvious, but we will see that there is more to gain: **1. Nc3+ Kb4 2. Nxd5+**. No matter where the Black king goes, the black rook is also in for it: **2. ... Ka4** or **Kc4 3. Nb6+ Kb5 4. Nxa8 Kc6** and Black will gain the knight in the corner as a consolation prize. After **2. ... Kb5 3. Nc7+ Kb6 4. Nxa8 Kb7**, Black will capture the knight a move quicker, but the loss will be the same: 11 points (queen and rook against a knight).

Targeting

In the diagram (⇧) a double attack is looming on a2. White's problem is that the queen cannot go from d4 to a2 in one move. After a move like **1. Qa1** Black can secure his bishop. However, White can gain time by attacking the rook on b8 with **1. Qa7**. Now Black has no time to bring his bishop into safety.

The queen move is an example of another type of preparatory move, called 'targeting'. The term 'targeting' is used for preparatory moves that prepare a double attack with tempo; that is, a piece attacks a particular target (e.g. the king, a piece, or a square) and at the same time threatens to initiate a double attack.

Targeting therefore involves gaining time; we call this a **gain of tempo**. A gain of tempo is an important weapon in chess.

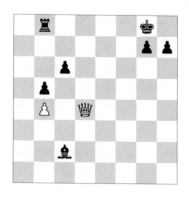

Preparatory moves that involve targeting are usually found in double attacks that feature pawns and knights.

In the left part of the diagram (⇨) White plays **1. c4** followed by **2. c5** winning a piece.

On the right, the knight first harries the rook: **1. Nf3 Rg2** (the rook is tied to the protection of the knight) **2. Nh4** (a move with two intentions) **2. ... Rg1 3. Rxg3+** (luring) **3. ... Rxg3 4. Nf5+**. White wins a piece.

The left part of the diagram (⇩) contains an illustrative example. White has the prospect of a knight fork on b5. With **1. Nd6+** White can get there with a gain of tempo. Black has no defence.

On the right, White seems to be doing okay. The black pawn is lost after 1. ... Rf8 2. e6. Unfortunately for White, Black has no need for the pawn. After **1. ... Ng5** the white position collapses. Black threatens to take on h7, and

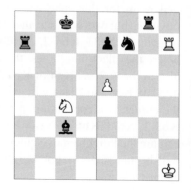

after **2. Rxe7 Nf3** White cannot escape mate. Another rook move doesn't help: **2. Rh2 Nf3 3. Rg2 Rh8+.**

In the diagram (⇑) we see a typical middlegame position. The unprotected bishop on c6 invites a tactical shot, as does the bishop on d6. In addition, White has an eye on g7. White can exploit the weaknesses in the black camp with a targeting move: after **1. Qd3 Rad8 2. Qc3** Black loses a piece.

To conclude this lesson, we discuss two nice examples which each involve a combination of preparatory moves.

In the diagram (⇨) White has a surprising way to regain the material that he is behind. **1. Rc3!** not only threatens to take the queen but also 2. Nd6#. Black is therefore forced to take the rook: **1. ... Qxc3**, after which it is harvest time: **2. Nd6+ Kc7 3. Nxb5+ Kc6 4. Nxc3.** Since White can easily stop Black's last pawn, the game will end in a draw.

The diagram (⇩) contains another example of a 'superfork'. White first eliminates one of the defending pawns and then continues to chase the black king around with his knight: **1. Qxa7+ Nxa7 2. Nb6+ Kb8 3. Nxd7+ Kc7 4. Nxf6** and White goes on to capture h5 on the next move. Step 4 students like these positions.

Search strategy
The search strategy for the exercise sheets is as follows:
- Can the king or another piece be chased to a square that invites a double attack?
- Is there a double attack, but no piece to execute it? Can such a piece be brought in with a gain of tempo?

The diagram (⇧) contains all the necessary ingredients for a double attack.
First the knight is brought into play with **1. ... Ng3+**. This prevents the king from going to g1 on account of **2. ... Ne2+**. White is also lost after **2. Kh2**. The type of preparatory move that is in order was introduced in lesson 3: **2. ... Qxe3 3. Qxe3 Nf1+**.
A combination of the preparatory moves chasing and luring.

PRACTICE

Reminder
◊ *Double attack: chasing and targeting*

Workbook

☐ *Double attack / Chasing or targeting: A*   ♖
Explanation: There are two ways to win material:

> Firstly, for the double attack to work, one of the targets must be forced to a particular square. The target can be forced to this square by means of chasing.
>
> Secondly, for the double attack to work, the piece that is to execute it must be played to a particular square. The piece can be played to that square with a gain of tempo.
>
> The arrangement of this exercise sheet is as follows:
> • 3x chasing + double attack with the knight
> • 3x targeting + double attack with the knight
> • 3x chasing + double attack with the queen
> • 3x targeting + double attack with the queen

Mistake: There is a mistake in an exercise that involves 'targeting'.
Help: Help should be provided only when the student fails to find the right move. In that case the exercise in question can be transformed into a Step 2 exercise by removing the queen or knight that is to execute the double attack. Where can this piece execute a double attack? How can this piece be played there with tempo from the original position?
Mistake: There is a mistake in an exercise that involves 'chasing'.
Help: Find an unprotected piece and try to set up a double attack that involves this piece.

□ *Double attack / Chasing or targeting: B* ♖ ♖

Explanation: See exercise sheet A. There is no specific arrangement.
Mistake: Position 12 is not solved correctly.
Help: This position is difficult. Study the position without the pawn
             on d6. In that case White has an easy win with 1. Rd7. With this
             information, the solution 1. Nc5 will no longer pose a problem.

ANSWERS

□ *Double attack / Chasing or targeting: A*
1) Drawing
2) 1. ... Qc5+ 2. Kf1 Ne3+; 2. Kh1
   Nf2+
3) 1. Nb6+ Kb8 2. Nd7+
4) 1. Nc7 and 2. Ne6+ or 2. Nxa8
5) 1. ... Nf3+ 2. Kxg2 Nd2
6) 1. ... Nc5 and 2. ... Nd3
7) 1. Qe8+ Kh7 2. Qe4+; 1. Qa8+?

   Rd8
8) 1. ... Qe1+ 2. Kg2 Qe4+; 1. ...
   Qe4+? 2. Qg2
9) 1. Qc2+ Kg8 2. Qc8+
10) 1. Qh5 g6 2. Qd5
11) 1. Qa4 b6 2. Qe4
12) 1. Qa7 and 2. Qa2+

□ *Double attack / Chasing or targeting: B*
1) 1. Qe5+ Kg8 2. Qd5+ winning a
   rook.
2) 1. Nf5 Qf6 2. Nh6+
3) 1. ... Bb7+ 2. Kg1 Ne2+
4) 1. Qb2 Rd1 2. Qb4+
5) 1. ... Qd4+ 2. Qf2 Qb4
6) 1. ... Qd1+ 2. Kg2 Qc2+

7) 1. f4 Re6 2. Ng7+
8) 1. ... Qd4+ 2. Be3 Qxb2
9) 1. Be3 Qa8 2. Nc7+
10) 1. ... Nd4 2. Qe3 Ne2+
11) 1. b4 Bd4 2. Qe4+
12) 1. Nc5! Re8 2. Na6; 1. ... dxc5 2.
    Rd7

13   Attacking the king

AIM OF THE LESSON
- learning to recognise a mating attack
- learning to execute a mating attack

PRIOR KNOWLEDGE
- tactical subjects
- mate by access, mating patterns

ACQUISITION

Instruction

We have already touched on the topic of 'attacking the king' in relation to a number of previous topics (mate in two by access, the magnet, etc.). It is a good idea to repeat these previous topics. More generally, it is important that the students recognise the relevant mating patterns. We therefore recommend that this lesson is done in combination with the three exercise sheets on mating patterns.

Access

Attacking the king often involves a castled king. This type of attack can be likened to an attack on a real castle. For such an attack to succeed, the defensive wall must be breached. Only then can the attacking pieces gain access to the king. In the diagram (⇩) White plays **1. Rxg7+** (breaching the wall) **1. ... Kxg7 2. Qg5+** (bringing in pieces) **2. ... Kh8 3. Qf6+ Kg8 4. Rg1 mate**. Note that threatening mate directly with 1. Qf6, 1. Qg5 or 1. Qh6 does not work, since Black can defend with 1. ... g6.

When it comes to attacking the king, three general rules apply:

- gain access
- bring in pieces (preferably by giving check, so as to proceed with tempo)
- give mate

Breaking through a castled position does not necessarily involve a capture. In the diagram (⇧) White can demolish the protective pawn shield with **1. Nf6+**. Black has to take, since 1. ... Kh8 is met by 2. Qh5#. After **1. ... gxf6** White gains access to the black king. White first brings in the queen with **2. Qg4+**, and after **2. ... Kh8** goes on to prepare the decisive rook jump with **3. Kg2**. Mate is inevitable.

Mating pattern
In order to correctly execute an attack on a castled king, a good knowledge of mating patterns is essential. Once the final position, i.e. a particular mating pattern, is known, the combination that is needed to get there is usually easy to find. This is true even if a queen sacrifice is in order, as in the diagram (⇨). White plays **1. Qf6** and after the forced **1. ... gxf6** gives mate with **2. Rg3+ Kh8 3. Bxf6#**. This mate with the rook and bishop is a characteristic mating pattern.

Learning to attack is a three-step process:

1) Exploiting a hole in the king's position.
If there is such a hole, bringing in additional pieces is essential. The diagram (⇩) contains a characteristic example of how to open a file and aim new pieces at the enemy king. With **1. Rf4** White forces the opening of the g-file. After **1. ... exf4 2. gxf4** (with the lethal threat of 3. Rg1+) **2. ... Kh8 3. Qxf6+** Black is mated.

2) Eliminating the defender
(capturing, luring away, chasing away, blocking and interfering)

85

Before capitalising on a weakened king, any defending pieces must first be eliminated.

In the left part of the diagram (⇧) White has already brought over half of his army to the black kingside. Nevertheless, White must still lure away the defending bishop that controls the d7-square. White achieves this with the help of a familiar blocking combination: **1. Rb7+ Bxb7 2. Nd7#**. Note that 1. Nd7+ Bxd7 leads to nothing.

On the right, the black king can still escape after the tempting 1. Qxh7+ Kf8. White can prevent this by playing **1. Bh6** first, after which mate is inevitable. Retaining the enemy king is an important attacking technique.

3) Creating a hole and bringing in pieces.
This technique has already been illustrated in the first three diagrams. In the left part of the diagram (⇨), White must refrain from opening up the position: after **1. Rb4** (1. Rxa7+ Kxa7 and the rook on b7 is not pinned any more), there is no defence against **2. Rxa7+** and **3. Ra4** mate. On the right, Black plays **1. ... Ng3+ 2. hxg3 Rf6**, with mate on h6 to follow.

In many cases a mating attack involves a combination of the points mentioned above. A typical attacking position is shown in the diagram (⇩). Ask the students to analyse the possibilities 1. Qxh7+, 1. Rh2 and 1. Qh6.
Of course, 1. Qxh7+ is met by 1. ... Kxh7 2. Rh2+ Kg8; 1. Rh2 h5 2. Qg5 is also insufficient on account of 2. ... Qa7+.
The correct move is **1. Qh6**. Black is forced to play **1. ... Rg8**, thus removing the only flight square available to his king. White can now play **2. Qxh7+** (not 2. Rh2? Qb6+ and Black plays the queen to d3 with check and then g5) **2. ... Kxh7 3. Rh2#**.

In the diagram (⇧) White's queen, rook and f-pawn already occupy menacing positions. Black's castled position is defended by the king and the f8-rook only. White decides the game with **1. f6 g6 2. Qg5** (threatening 3. Qh6 with mate on the next move) **2. ... Kh8 3. Qh6 Rg8 4. Qxh7+** (or the less pretty but equally sufficient **4. Rh3**).

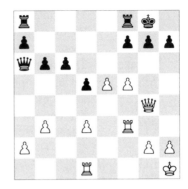

Reminder
◊ *Attacking the castled king*

Workbook

☐ *Attacking the king / Mating pattern (♖♗): A*   ♖
  Explanation: The first three diagrams contain mating patterns that have been taken from the exercises. In each case there is a forced mate in three. Exercises in which the goal is mate are all about recognizing the mating pattern concerned. When mating the king, the students should make use of familiar motifs such as double check, access, the different forms of eliminating the defender and, last but not least, preparatory luring and chasing moves.
  Mistake: An occasional mistake is likely. If the exercises are too difficult, the student should tackle easier exercises first.
  Help: Determine the nature of the mistake and ask the student to try once more.

☐ *Attacking the king / Mating pattern (♖♘): B*   ♖
  Explanation: See exercise A.

☐ *Attacking the king / Mating pattern (♗♘): C*   ♖
  Explanation: See exercise A.

☐ *Attacking the king / Weakness: A*   ♖
  Explanation: The attack on the king is in an advanced stage. A hole has already been created in the enemy's castled position. Mate can be achieved by executing a familiar (mating) combination and by bringing in extra pieces.

The students may require board and pieces for these exercises. By their nature some of these exercises are up to four moves deep.

Mistake: The attack is not successful.

Help: Set up the position and play it to a finish. Why is the attack unsuccessful? Is it because of a defender? Then eliminate it! Is it because of insufficient material? Then bring in some extra pieces!

☐ *Attacking the king / Access:* ♝　　　♜ ♜

Explanation: In these exercises the attacker can break open, i.e. gain access to, the enemy's castled position with a sacrifice. Finishing the mating attack takes one extra move. Nearly all of the exercises lead to mate quickly.

Mistake: There is still a defence.

Help: The exercises should not be done too hastily. In position 6, for example, the hasty 1. Nh6+ Kh8 2. Bxf6 is incorrect on account of 2. ... exf3. In position 9, 1. Rxh7 Kxh7 2. Qg4 does not win, since Black still has 2. ... f6. The students should find these defences themselves, and then try their hand at these positions once more.

☐ *Attacking the king / Elimination of the defence:* ♝　♜ ♜ ♜

Explanation: The attack on the king cannot be executed yet, since there is an important defender which has to be eliminated first. The types of eliminating the defender that are featured on this sheet include capturing, luring away, chasing away and interfering. A useful technique to eliminate a defender is to pin (and, if necessary, capture) it. This sheet is more difficult than the previous one.

Mistake: The attack is not properly followed up.

Help: Ask the student to find the important defender. How can this defender be eliminated?

ANSWERS

☐ *Attacking the king / Mating pattern (♖♗): A*
1) 4 mating patterns
2) 4 mating patterns
3) 4 mating patterns
4) 1. ... Qxf1+ 2. Kxf1 Bd3+
5) 1. Rf3+ Kh8 2. Ng6+ hxg6 3. Rh3#
6) 1. Qxg8+ Kxg8 2. Rh8+
7) 1. ... Rxh2+ 2. Qxh2 Qxh2+ 3. Kxh2 Rh8#
8) 1. Ne7+ Kh8 2. Ng6+
9) 1. Qa8+ Kh7 2. Qh8+
10) 1. Ra8+ Kxa8 2. Bxc7 gxh3 3. Ra1#
11) 1. Qxd4 Bxd4 2. Bxd4 b5 3. Rh8#
12) 1. Be6+ Kb7 2. Bd5+ Ka7 3. Ra8#; 1. Bd5+ Qxh8

☐ *Attacking the king / Mating pattern (♖♘): B*
1) 4 mating patterns
2) 4 mating patterns
3) 4 mating patterns
4) 1. Qxh7+ Kxh7 2. Rh3+
5) Drawing
6) Drawing
7) 1. Ne7+ Kh8 2. Qxh7+
8) 1. Ndf7+ Kh7 2. Ng5+
9) 1. Qxh6+ Bxh6 2. Ng5+ Kh8 3. Rh7#
10) 1. Qg6 fxg6 2. Rxg7+
11) 1. ... Qh3 2. Rbg1 Qxh2+
12) 1. Qxg7+ Nxg7 2. Rxh6+

☐ *Attacking the king / Mating pattern (♗♘): C*
1) 4 mating patterns
2) 4 mating patterns
3) 4 mating patterns
4) 1. ... Qb4+ 2. Ka1 Qc3+
5) 1. ... Qxg2+ 2. Kxg2 Bf3+
6) 1. Qxh7+ Nxh7 2. Ng6+
7) 1. Ng6+ Kh7 2. Ne5+
8) 1. Qxc7+ Kxc7 2. Nd5+
9) 1. ... Qxg2 2. Kxg2 Nf4+
10) 1. Nef6+ gxf6 2. Bh6+
11) 1. Qf6 gxf6 2. Nh6+
12) 1. Qg8+ Kxg8 2. Ne7+

☐ *Attacking the king / Weakness: A*
1) 1. Bxh7+ Kh8 2. Bg6+ Kg8 3. Qh7+ Kf8 4. Qxf7#
2) 1. Qg7+ Bxg7 2. Bxg7+ Kg8 3. Bf6#
3) 1. Qg7+ Bxg7 2. Rd8+ Bf8 3. Rxf8#
4) 1. Bh6+ Kxh6 2. Qf6+ Kh5 3. g4#
5) 1. Qg3 Rg8 2. Qc3+
6) 1. Rf4 exf4 2. gxf4 and 3. Rg1
7) 1. … Ng3 2. Kg1 Qg2+ 3. Rxg2 Nh3#
8) 1. Bf6
9) 1. Ng4 fxg4 2. Bxh7+ with mate as in position 1.
10) 1. Qh6 Qe7 (protects f7; see 1) 2. Qxh7+ Kf8 3. Qh8#
11) 1. Qxf7 Nxf7 2. Rg8+ Rxg8 3. Nxf7#
12) 1. Qg4+ Kh8 2. Qh4

89

□ *Attacking the king / Access:* **B**
1) 1. Nf6+ gxf6 2. Qg3+ Kh8 3. Bxf6#
2) 1. Qxh7+ Rxh7 2. Rg8+ and mate; 1. ... Kxh7 2. Rh5#
3) 1. Ng6+ hxg6 2. Qh6+ Bh7 3. Qxg7#
4) 1. Ne7+ Kh8 2. Rxh7+ Kxh7 3. Qh1#; 2. ... Nxh7 3. Ng6#
5) 1. Ng6+ fxg6 2. Qxh7+ Kxh7 3. Rh4#
6) 1. Nh6+ gxh6 2. Qxf6; 1. ... Kh8 2. Qxf6!; 2. Bxf6? exf3

7) Drawing
8) Drawing
9) 1. Qh5 Bh4 2. Qxh7+ Kxh7 3. Rxh4+ Kg8 4. Rh8#; 1. ... gxh5 2. Rg3+ and mate.
10) 1. Qg6 hxg5 (1. ... fxg6 2. Ne7+ Kh8 3. Nxg6+) 2. hxg5 fxg6 3. Ne7#
11) 1. Qxh7+ Kxh7 2. Rh5+ Kg7 3. Bh6+ Kh8 4. Bf8#
12) 1. Qc7+ Ka7 2. Qxb7+ Kxb7 3. Rb3+ Ka7 4. Rc7#

□ *Attacking the king / Elimination of the defence:* **C**
1) 1. ... Ne2+ 2. Rxe2 Nf4
2) 1. Qxg7+ Kxg7 2. Rh8! and 3. R1h7#
3) 1. Re8 Qxe8 2. Qxf6+; 1. ... Bc4 2. Qg7#
4) 1. Qh6 Rg8 2. Re8 Qxe8 3. Qf6+
5) 1. Nf6+ Bxf6 2. Bd3
6) 1. Nf5 fxg5 2. Ne7#
7) 1. Re7 Rxe7 2. Qxf8#; 1. ... Bxe7

2. Qxh7#
8) 1. Bxh7+ Nxh7 2. Qxf7+ Kh8 3. Ng6#
9) 1. Rg3+ Kh8 2. Re4; 1. Re4? Qg7
10) 1. Rf5 and 2. Qh6
11) 1. Rxd7 Bxd7 2. Nf6+ Kf8 3. Nd5
12) 1. Qf6 Bxf6 (otherwise 2. Rh8+) 2. gxf6 and 3. Rh8#

14   Seventh rank

AIM OF THE LESSON
- learning new tactical possibilities
- exploiting the 7ᵗʰ rank

PRIOR KNOWLEDGE
- mating patterns

ACQUISITION

Instruction

We start this lesson by repeating some 'mate in two' exercises in which a rook on the 7ᵗʰ rank plays an important part.

All it takes to show the strength of a rook on the 7ᵗʰ rank is a diagram (⇨) with a white rook on e7 and the black king on g8. The king is tied to the back rank. Note, too, that a rook on the 7ᵗʰ rank cannot be attacked by pawns (but if they are there the rook can capture them) and so has to cope with fewer defenders.

The cramping effect of a rook on the 7ᵗʰ rank can be exploited for both tactical and positional ends. The tactical ends usually involve mate. In some cases, however, a rook on the 7ᵗʰ rank can be used to gain material or escape with a draw.

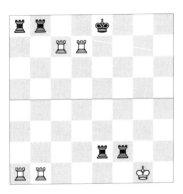

We first look at two typical examples that illustrate the attacking possibilities of two rooks on the 7ᵗʰ rank. The upper part of the diagram (⇩) contains an elementary position. White has mate in three after **1. Rh7** (threatening mate on h8) **1. ... Kd8 2. Rcg7**, with mate on the next move. In the lower part, this strategy does not work because there is not enough room between the king and the corner square. Hence, there is no mate; after **1. ... Rh2 2. Rd1 Rdg2+ 3. Kf1 Rb2 4. Kg1** White defends himself. In this case, then, the king is safer on the wing than in the centre. Away from the centre, the rooks need a little help from a friend.

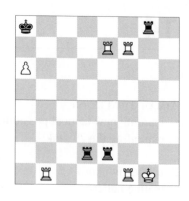

Mate with support
In the diagram (⇧) White has two rooks on the 7th rank and a pawn on a6. White wins after **1. Rb7+ Ka8 2. Ra7+ Kb8 3. Rfb7+ Kc8 4. Ra8#**.

Sometimes help is provided not by one's own pieces, but by an enemy piece. This is the case in the lower part of the diagram, where the castled rook is still on f1. Black plays **1. ... Rg2+ 2. Kh1 Rh2+ 3. Kg1 Rdg2#**. The king is trapped between the edge of the board and his own rook, which is blocking the flight path. A quite common mate.

The above examples show that the rooks on the 7th rank can be assisted in two ways:
• by one's own pieces
• by the opponent's pieces
Both have typical combinations associated to them.

In the diagram (⇨) White controls the 7th rank, but cannot give mate yet. White must first play **1. Qxf8+** (1. Qf7? Rd1+). After **1. ... Rxf8** White has eliminated the defender of h7 and the rook on f8 is now blocking the black king's escape route. The majority of combinations that are based on the 7th rank involve eliminating the defender.

In the diagram (⇩), the rooks on the 7th rank cannot give mate on their own. Therefore White first plays **1. Rh7+ Kg8 2. Reg7+ Kf8** so as to get in the knight with **3. Nf5** (or 3. Nxh5), which provides support on the 7th rank. There is no defence against the mating threat **4. Rh8#**.

Another characteristic 7th rank combination is one in which material is won by means of a repeated discovered check.

In the diagram (⇧) the battery of rook and bishop proves to be an all-destructive force. The black king has to move back into the discovered check time and time again. In the meantime White picks off Black's pieces one by one: **1. Rxf7+ Kg8 2. Rg7+ Kh8 3. Rxd7+ Kg8 4. Rg7+ Kh8 5. Rxc7+ Kg8 6. Rg7+ Kh8 7. Rxb7+ Kg8 8. Rg7+ Kh8 9. Rc7+ Kg8 10. Rxc8**. White has won a total of 19 points. Note that White recharged the battery of rook and bishop on every move. This was possible because the black king has nowhere to go.

The black king is equally powerless in the diagram (⇨). White first introduces a mating threat: **1. Ra7+ Kb8 2. Rcb7+ Kc8 3. Rxf7**. Now the only way for Black to prevent 4. Ra8# is to retreat his king: **3. ... Kb8 4. Rfb7+ Kc8 5. Rxg7**. The recurrent mating threat gives White the opportunity to clear the 7th rank: **5. ... Kb8 6. Rgb7+ Kc8 7. Rh7 Rxh7 8. Rxh7** and White wins.

The position in the diagram (⇩) is taken from the game *Anand-Kamsky, New Delhi 1990*. White would love to get his two rooks to the 7th rank, but after 1. gxf5 Rxf6 2. Rd1 Kg8 3. Rd8+ Rf8 4. Rdd7 Rxf5 this will not be sufficient. Instead, Anand played the very powerful **1. Rd1**. With this move White retains the strong knight (1. ... Rxf6 2. Rd8+ and mate). Black's bishop now has to give up the control of d7 (the pawn on h7 needs protection to prevent mate). The game continued **1. ... Bg6** (1. ... Be4 2. f3 is the same) **2. Rdd7** and all Black

93

can do to postpone mate is give a couple of innocent checks.

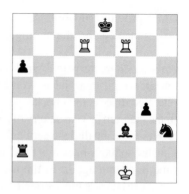

Perpetual check
In the diagram (⇑) White again has two rooks on the 7th rank, but this time his situation is less enviable. With his rook on the 2nd rank, Black has the better chances. The immediate threat is mate on a1. White must use the good position of his rooks to give perpetual check. Ask the students to find out with which rook they should give check. The correct rook is the f-rook. If the d-rook gives the checks, Black will move his king to b8, after which White will have run out of checks.

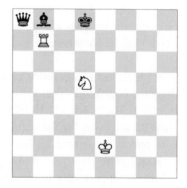

In the diagram (⇨) White must also try to draw the game. He can achieve this by setting up a familiar drawing mechanism with rook and knight. White must first bring his rook and knight into position with the help of a luring tactic: **1. Rd7+! Ke8** (1. … Kc8? 2. Nb6# or 1. … Kxd7 2. Nb6+) **2. Nf6+**.
This position, which was discussed in Step 3, should be memorised by all the students, since it occurs very frequently (also with the king cut off on the a- or h-file). The knight gives check and protects the rook at the same time. Black has to move away with his king: **2. … Kf8 3. Nh7+ Kg8 4. Nf6+**. Black is forced to go back to f8 (4. … Kh8 5. Rh7#), and so White has a perpetual.

Search strategy
The rook on the 7th rank must be assisted by other pieces. The task is thus to either bring in new troops or eliminate defenders. In the diagram (⇩) the h-pawn prevents the queen from taking part. At Step 4 level, a student should not miss the sacrifice on h7. After **1. Nxh7 Nxh7 2. Qg6** Black cannot avoid being mated on g7.

Reminder
◊ *Seventh rank*

Workbook

☐ *Tactics / Seventh rank: A* ♖
Explanation: A rook on the 7th rank is the pride and joy of the position. In one position, the win involves eliminating the defender which is preventing mate. In some other positions, mate is made possible with the 'assistance' of enemy pieces.
Mistake: The suggested solution is incorrect.
Help: No help is necessary. Check the mistake and ask the student to try once more.
Mistake: The suggested answer for position 12 is 1. d6.
Help: Ask the student to find the correct defence (1. ... Ne8). Provide the correct answer if necessary.

☐ *Tactics / Seventh rank: B* ♖ ♖
Explanation: See the A-sheet.
Mistake: The suggested answer for position 10 is 1. Ne6.
Help: While this is a good idea, Black can defend with 1. ... Re7. How can this idea be improved upon?
Mistake: Position 12 is too difficult.
Help: The students should discover that the queen is tied to the protection of the d1-rook.

☐ *Tactics / Seventh rank: A*
1) 1. Qf1+ Ke8 2. Qb5+ Kf8 3. Qxc5+
2) 1. Rb7+ Ka8 2. Qxc8+ Rxc8 3. Rxa7+ Kb8 4. Rhg7#
3) 1. Ra7+ Kb8 2. Rcb7+ Kc8 3. a6
4) 1. ... Rxb2 2. Qxa8+ Ke7
5) 1. ... Qe3 2. Rxf2 Qxh3+ 3. Kg1 Qg3+
6) 1. ... Qxe4+! 2. Nxe4 Nf3; 1. ...

Nf3? 2. Qxh7#
7) 1. Nf6+ Kh8 2. Qxh6+; 1. ... gxf6 2. Qe6+ Kh8 3. Qxf6+; 1. Qxh6? b1Q!
8) 1. ... Rg2 2. a8Q Rbf2 3. Ke1 Rg1#
9) 1. ... Nf3 2. gxf3 Rd2
10) 1. Qxg6 fxg6 2. Rxg7+ Kh8 3. Rh7+ Kg8 4. Rag7#

11) 1. Qxf4+ Nxf4 2. Rcf7+ Ke8 3. Rg8#

12) 1. Nxf6+ exf6 2. Re7; 1. d6!? Ne8!

□ *Tactics / Seventh rank: B*
1) 1. ... Qxd4+ 2. Qxd4 Rg2+ 3. Kh1 Rxh2+ 4. Kg1 Rbg2#
2) 1. Rg7+ Kh8 2. Nf8 (threatens 3. Ng6#) 2. ... Rxf8 3. Rh7+ Kg8 4. Rcg7#
3) 1. Nf6 Bg7 2. Qh6 and 3. Qxh7# or 3. Rxh7#
4) 1. Rxg7+ Kxg7 2. Rc7+
5) 1. Qd7 Qh8 (otherwise 2. Rf8+) 2. Rh7 Qf6 3. Rh8+
6) 1. c8Q Rxc8 2. Qb7; 1. ... Qxb2 2. Qc7; 1. Qb7? Re2 or 1. ... Rc8
7) Drawing
8) Drawing
9) 1. ... Rf8 2. Qxd2 Rxd2+
10) 1. Nf5! (1. Ne6 Re7); 1. ... gxf5 2. Rd7
11) 1. Bh6 gxh6 2. R1e7; 1. ... Rg8 2. R1e7
12) 1. ... Be3! 2. fxe3 Qh3+; 2. Qxe3 Qxd1; 2. Nc2 Qf3

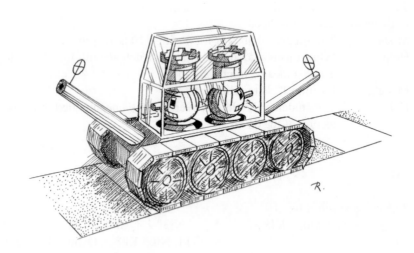

15   Endgame strategy

• learning how to plan in the endgame

PRIOR KNOWLEDGE
• square of the pawn
• key squares

ACQUISITION

Instruction
Some of the principles of endgame play are specific to endgames and do not play a role in the opening and middlegame. In this lesson we discuss a number of general endgame principles using the pawn ending as example.

The pawn ending in the diagram (⇨) is winning for White on account of his extra pawn. The road to victory consist of giving up the a-pawn in exchange for time. Here is a possible variation: **1. a5 Kc6 2. Ke5 Kb5 3. Kd6 Kxa5 4. Ke7 f5 5. Kf7 g5 6. Kg7 h5 7. Kg6 g4 8. Kxf5** and White collects all of Black's pawns. White has given up a pawn to gain time and to get at the black pawns more quickly. The black king was lured away by the white a-pawn.

The distant passed pawn
In the diagram (⇩) material is even. Once again, White can gain time by giving up his a-pawn. After **1. a5+ Kxa5 2. Kxc5** White's king is closer to the black kingside pawns.
In the starting position White's a-pawn is farther removed from the kingside pawns than Black's c-pawn. White therefore has what is called the distant passed pawn. Having the distant passed

pawn is a great advantage.

In endgames, 3 elements have to be weighed against each other continuously:
- Is my king active?
- Can I create a passed pawn?
- Is my opponent threatening anything?

Each move must be determined on the basis of the relative importance of these elements.
We now consider the diagram (⇧) and try to weigh the points under a) an b) against each other.
White's king can go to the centre and he can create a passed pawn. We let White try the latter first: 1. b5 axb5 2. axb5 Kc7 3. Kd2 Kb6 4. Kd3 Kxb5 5. Kd4 Kc6 and Black's king is back in time. Next we let White activate his king first: **1. Kd2 Kd7 2. Kd3 Kd6 3. Kd4 Kc6 4. f4 Kd6 5. b5 axb5 6. axb5 Kc7 7. Kd5 Kb6 8. Kd6 Kxb5 9. Ke7 g5 10. f5** and White has an easy win.

The latter approach is similar to that in the first diagram of this lesson. Make sure to show the whole variation on the board.
The situation in the diagram (⇨) is rather different. Black has two passed pawns already, and so it is too late for White to activate his king. Much more effective is **1. b6** (or **1. a6**) **1. ... axb6 2. a6**, and White queens.

How to create a passed pawn?
Creating a passed pawn should be done with care and involves more than just advancing pawns. In the diagram (⇩) White can create a passed pawn on the queenside. At first sight, the move 1. a3, with the aim of following up with 2. b4, looks attractive. Unfortunately, 1. a3 can be met by 1. ... a4, after which Black fixes the white majority and wins! Ask the students to discover this themselves. Black has more than one road

to victory. The nicest is to 'stalemate' the white king on f1 and force a move with the b-pawn. That is why White should start with **1. b3**. After **1. ... Kg6 2. a3 Kf6 3. b4** Black is without a chance. The b-pawn is the 'candidate' passed pawn. The rule is: the candidate first!

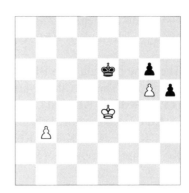

The protected passed pawn
Another strategic advantage is to have a protected passed pawn. In the diagram (⇑) White's king is forced to remain within the square of the h-pawn. As such he is unable to support his own pawn. Black has all the time in the world to collect the b-pawn.

Defending options
It is important not to lose one's options. In the left part of the diagram (⇨) White seems to be lost. However, White has **1. Ka5**, giving Black the choice between stalemate after **1. ... Kxc5** or losing a pawn (with a draw).
On the right, the h-pawn is in danger. If Black can take it on h4, his king will occupy a key square. White can escape with **1. h5**. After **1. ... gxh5 2. Ke2 Kg3 3. Kf1** the White king reaches the corner or he closes in the Black king after **3. ... Kh2 4. Kf2**. In both cases the game will end in a draw.

Zugzwang
One rather difficult technique that plays a role in some pawn endings is that of Zugzwang. In Zugzwang positions it is a drawback to be the one to move. In such cases the best option would be to pass, but this, of course, is not allowed.

The diagram (⇩) contains a tricky position in which it is essential to choose the right strategy. As White, it is tempting to attack the black pawn and protect the pawn on c4. If he does this, however, he will be lost after **1. Kb5 Kd4**.

Using the concept of Zugzwang White will emerge victorious: **1. Kb6 Kd4 2. Kb5**.

The same position with Black to move is also interesting. There are three variations. Winning is **1. ... Kd3! 2. Kb5 Kd4**. Losing would be 1. ... Kd4 2. Kb5, while the game is drawn after 1. ... Ke5 2. Kb6! Kd6 3. Kb5 Kd7! 4. Kxc5 Kc7. A useful revision of key squares!

In the diagram (⇧) the g-pawn is still in its initial position. This type of pawn is a valuable asset in Zugzwang positions, since it affords White the choice between a single or a double step forward. This is a perfect way to avoid being in Zugzwang.
Ask the students to find out whether White should start with 1. g4 or 1. g3. A single step forward leads to a win; a double step forward leads to a draw.

Keeping the king at a distance
The technique of shielding off the king, as was discussed in the lesson on key squares in Step 3, remains a convenient weapon.
In the diagram (⇨) White must start with **1. Kb5**. The black king has to move away, after which **1. ... Kxa2 2. Kb6** wins easily. An instructive variation is the incorrect 1. Kb6 Kb4! (not 1. ... Ka4 2. a3 with zugzwang) 2. a3+ Ka4 and White does not have a good move any more.

In the diagram (⇩), we see a similar scenario. White wins with **1. Kf5** (shielding off) **1. ... Kg2 2. Kg6**.

The aim of this lesson has been to provide a first step towards planning in the endgame. To this end, we introduced 3 general endgame rules, which we illustrated against the backdrop of a number of pawn endings.

Reminder
◊ *Strategy in pawn endings*

☐ **Workbook**

☐ *Endgame strategy / Pawn ending: A* ♖
Explanation: Ask the students to write down more than the moves only; they should add why a particular position is winning or a draw (e.g. king on a key square, king outside the square of the pawn). Some positions can also be played to a finish; in that case the trainer plays against one student first and then moves on to the next.
Mistake: The suggested answer is wrong.
Help: Help is required only when the student cannot himself find the mistake. In that case it is advisable to play the position to a finish using the right move, and to discuss the position with the student afterwards.

☐ *Test / Mix: G* ♖
Explanation: Most of the topics on this exercise sheet have been taken from previous lessons (chasing and aiming, attack on the king, 7th rank)

☐ *Test / Mix: H* ♖♖
Explanation: The themes on this exercise sheet have been taken from all previous lessons. Solving these exercises requires the students to recognize the characteristics of the positions. It is a good idea to discuss the first three exercises on the demonstration board, emphasizing the correct search strategy.

ANSWERS

☐ *Endgame strategy / Pawn ending: A*

1) 1. h4 Kd4 2. f6 (putting in place an obstacle; the black king must remain outside of the square of the pawn)
2) 1. a4 Kc5 2. a5 (the pawns hem in the king; White captures on h3 and then approaches with the king)
3) 1. g3 g5 2. g4 Kc6 3. Kxc4; 1. g4? g5 (making use of zugzwang)
4) 1. a5 bxa5 2. Kd2 Kb3 3. Kc1 (changing the pattern of key squares by giving Black a rook's pawn)
5) 1. ... Kb8 activate the king first.

(1. ... b5 2. axb6+ only draws, the white king will come to c1 in time)

6) 1. ... b6 2. Kf3 a6 (advance the candidate passed pawn first)

7) 1. ... Kc3 2. a4 Kxd4 3. Ke6 Kc5 4. Ke5 Kb4 with a draw (shield off the king first)

8) 1. ... g5+ 2. hxg5 Kg6 (weaken the pawn structure first)

9) 1. ... a6 2. Kd2 Kb3 (prevent b5 and then activate the king)

10) 1. ... f5 (prevent e4 first and then activate the king)

11) 1. ... f4 2. Kc4 Kg6 (activating the king; 1. ... Kg6 first is met by 2. g3)

12) 1. ... h4 (1. ... Kg4 2. Kh6 Kxg3 3. Kxh5) 2. gxh4 h5 (shielding off the king)

□ *Test / Mix: G*

1) 1. Qb8+ Kh7 2. Qb1+ (double attack: chasing)

2) 1. Ne6 Bxe3 2. Nxd8+ (discovered attack)

3) 1. ... Rxc3 2. Rxa2 Rf3+ (7th rank)

4) 1. Qg1+ Kf8 2. Qc1 (double attack: targeting)

5) 1. Rg1+ Kh8 2. Qxh7+ Kxh7 3. Rh4# (mate through access)

6) 1. Rc7+ Kg6 2. Qd1 (double attack: chasing)

7) 1. ... Re2 2. Qxc5 Rgxg2+; 2. Rxg5 Rxf2 3. Rxf2 hxg5 (7th rank)

8) 1. Qg6 Bxg3 2. f6 (attack on the king)

9) 1. Rg4+ fxg4 2. Qg6+ Kh8 3. Qh7# (attack on the king: gaining access)

10) 1. h3 Nh6 2. Qe4 (double attack: eliminating the defender)

11) 1. ... Qxg2+ 2. Rxg2 Rdxg2+ 3. Kh1 Rg1+ (7th rank)

12) 1. Qh5 Nc6 2. Qh2+ (double attack: targeting)

□ *Test / Mix: H*

1) 1. Ra8+ Bd8 2. Rxd8+ Kxd8 3. Nxf7+ (double attack: luring)

2) Drawing

3) 1. Bf8 Rxf8 2. Ne7# (mate)

4) 1. e4 Bxe4 2. Qb1 (placing the front piece)

5) 1. Rxf6 Qxf6 2. Qc2; 1. Qc2? Rc4 (double attack: eliminating the defender)

6) 1. Qxg6+ hxg6 2. Nf6+ Kg7 3. Rh7# (attack on the king: gaining access)

7) 1. d6 Bxd6 2. Qd2 (double attack: luring)

8) 1. Rf6 Qxe5 2. Qxh6+; 2. Rh6+? Kg8 (attack on the king)

9) 1. ... Qxh2+ 2. Kxh2 Nf3+ and 3. ... Nf2# (double check: luring)

10) 1. ... Qg3 2. fxg3 Rxg2+ 3. Kh1 Rdd2 (7th rank)

11) 1. Bg6+ Kxg6 2. Qh5#; 1. ... Ke6 2. Qc8+ Qd7 3. Bf5+ (double attack: chasing)

12) 1. ... Bxf2+ 2. Kxf2 Nxe4+; 2. Qxf2 Nd3+ (double attack: luring)

16   Clearing

AIM OF THE LESSON
- learning tactical skills

PRIOR KNOWLEDGE
- double attack

ACQUISITION

Instruction

The fifth and last type of preparatory move that sets up a double attack is the 'clearing' of a line (file, rank or diagonal) or a square. A clearing move involves moving away a piece of your own army, thereby preparing a double attack.

Clearing with check

In the left part of the diagram (⇨) the queen on b3 has to make way for the double attack to work. It is important that the queen move is with tempo. This can best be done by giving check. Black therefore plays **1. ... Qa4+** and after **2. Na3** picks up the queen with **2. ... Nb3+**. On the right, the gain of tempo also involves check. Black's **1. ... Qh5+** sets up **2. ... Ng5**, winning an exchange.

The diagram (⇩) contains some examples of clearing that involve pieces other than the queen. On the left, a clearing move with the knight sets up a pawn fork. It goes without saying that the knight should be played to a6: **1. Na6+ Kb7 2. b4**.

On the right, the king on h2 and the rook on d6 are placed on the same diagonal. The black bishop can fork the two if the knight is moved away first. After **1. ... Ng4+ 2. hxg4 Be5+** Black picks up the exchange.

Clearing with a capture

Another way to gain a tempo is by means of a capture. Capturing in most cases forces the opponent to recapture; the time it takes to do this can be used to set up a double attack.
In the left part of the diagram (⇧) White can clear square c4 with **1. Bxa6**. White wins a piece after **1. ... bxa6** and **2. Rc4**.

In the right part we see a similar position. Note, however, that 1. ... Qh4+ can be met by 2. Kg1. The correct move is **1. ... Qxf4**. White loses a piece, regardless of whether he takes on f4 or not.

Clearing with an attack

Clearing with a gain of tempo can also be done by attacking an enemy piece that is unprotected or insufficiently protected.
A simple illustration is provided in the left part of the diagram (⇨). White can clear the b4- square by means of **1. Nd5**, after which he threatens both **2. Nxc7** and **2. b4**. Either way Black will lose material.
On the right, the clearing move **1. Nf4** also wins material. If the bishop moves, White picks up a rook with **2. Kg6**.

In the diagram (⇩) we can see a remarkable example of clearing. If it were not for the queen, White would have a knight fork on f8. This suggests that White should try to clear the f8-square. However, this is easier said than done, since the queen neither has a suitable attacking target, nor does she seem able to protect the pinned knight. White does not win after 1. Qxg7+? Qxg7 2. Nxg7 Kxg7 3. Kg4 Kf7 4. Kg5 Kg7 5. h5 gxh5 6. Kxh5 Kf6 7. Kg4 Kg6. But White has the surprising **1. Qf5** up his sleeve. This move not only protects the knight and releases it from the pin, but it also clears f8: **1. ... gxf5** is met by **2. Nf8+**, and White wins.

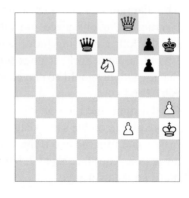

Line clearance

Besides clearing a square it is also possible to clear a line (i.e. a file, rank or diagonal). Clearing a line involves moving away a piece with a gain of tempo, thereby setting up a double attack. Here, too, the tempo can be gained by giving check or by attacking an enemy piece.

In the upper part of the diagram (⇧) White can win the rook on c8 with **1. f6 Bxf6 2. Qg4+**. With the first move White clears the h3/c8 diagonal. This preparatory move is necessary, because the direct 1. Qg4+ can be met by 1. ... Bg5.

In the lower part of the diagram, the bishop on e3 obstructs a double attack of the rook. White clears the e3-square with tempo by **1. Bg1** and picks up an exchange. Note, again, that White cannot do without a preparatory move. After the immediate 1. Rd3+ Black can save himself with 1. ... Kc2.

In the diagram (⇨) Black's knight on e5 hems in the bishop on g7. Black clears the bishop's diagonal by capturing on f3 with check. Now, all of a sudden, two attacking targets have become available. White loses a piece after **1. ... Nxf3+ 2. Bxf3 Qf6**. It seems as though Black can also win a piece with Qb4. However, in that case White can escape with 2. Ne4!

Double attacks can also arise in the opening phase. After the moves **1. e4 c5 2. Nf3 Nc6 3. c3 d6 4. Be2 Nf6 5. d4 Nxe4** we arrive at the position in the diagram (⇩). Black's last move is a well-known mistake. White can win a piece with **6. d5**. The pawn chases the knight away and at the same time clears the 4th rank. After **6. ... Ne5, 7. Qa4+** picks up the knight on e4. This trap is found in a number of openings and has claimed many a victim over the years.

Queens, rooks and bishops are line pieces. As a consequence, they often take part in double attacks that involve clearing moves. But sometimes a knight fork can also be set up by means of clearing. In such cases, the help of a pin is usually required.

In the diagram (⇑) White wins the exchange with **1. Nxf5 gxf5 2. Nd4**, regardless of whether Black takes on d4. Below, we will also see an example of a clearing move that sets up a double attack for a pawn (cf the second position under Search strategy).

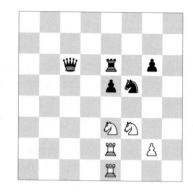

Search strategy

The search strategy for the exercises focuses on opportunities for a double attack. Targets include unprotected pieces and open kings. The piece that obstructs the double attack must be played away with a gain of tempo.

In the first diagram (⇨) we see an example of square clearing. One likely target is the rook on h8, which is unprotected. A second target is harder to find. The e7-square is a possible mating square, since the queen can be lured away with Nxc6. Unfortunately, the rook on a7 also protects e7. Luring away the queen does set up a double attack, however. With **1. Nxc6** White does not only clear d4 for the queen, but also lures the queen away from the protection of the rook. After **1. ... Qxc6** White attacks both rooks with **2. Qd4**.

The second example, shown in the diagram (⇩), involves line clearing. Black has just protected his pawn on b7 with Na5. The drawback of this move is that it invites a pawn fork on b4. White's problem is that his rook is in the way. The solution is simple: the rook clears the b-file and attacks the black queen in the process. After **1. Rh3 Qg6** White wins a piece with **2. b4**.

106

Reminder

◊ *Double attack: clearing*

Workbook

□ *Double attack / Clearing: A* ♖

Explanation: The position already contains a double attack. All it takes is to move away the obstructing piece with gain of tempo.

Mistake: The suggested move does not win any material.

Help: Explain the goal of the exercise. Ask supporting questions but let the student draw his own conclusions. If necessary, take away the obstructing piece. This reduces the exercise to a Step 2 level exercise.

Mistake: Position 8 is too difficult.

Help: This exercise does not only involve clearing, but also chasing away (i.e. the rook on g3).

□ *Double attack / Clearing: A* ♖♖

Explanation: The goal is to set up X-ray checks and attacks by means of any of the five preparatory moves (luring, chasing, aiming, eliminating the defender and clearing).

Mistake: The position is too difficult.

Help: Provide the type of preparatory move that is required.

☐ *Double attack / Clearing: A*

1) 1. Nxc6 Rxc6 2. Qd4+
2) 1. Qa8+ Kh7 2. Nf3
3) 1. ... Nxf3+ 2. gxf3 Qd4+
4) 1. g5 Bg7 2. Qh3+; 1. Qh3+? Kg8 2. g5 Bf5
5) 1. Bxd5 Nxd5 2. Nc6
6) 1. Qxf5 Rxf5 2. Ne6+

7) 1. ... Qxf3+ 2. Bxf3 Ne3+
8) 1. ... Nf5 2. Rf3 Qb8+; 1. ... Qb8? 2. Be5
9) 1. Rxc3 bxc3 2. g4
10) 1. e6 fxe6 2. Qc3; 1. Qc3? Bb4
11) 1. ... Bb3 2. Re1 Nc4
12) 1. ... b3 2. axb3 Nb4

☐ *Double attack / X-ray: A*

1) 1. Qxd6 Rxd6 2. Bb4
2) 1. e4 dxe4 2. Bg4; 1. Bg4? Qb1+
3) 1. ... d4 2. Bxd4 Bd5+
4) 1. ... f5 2. Nd2 Bb4
5) 1. ... Re5+ 2. Kc4 Be2+; 2. Kc6 Bd7#
6) 1. ... Rb1 2. Qxb1 Qh1+
7) 1. ... Nc6+ 2. Bxc6 Rb1+

8) 1. ... Nf5 2. exf5 Rh2+
9) 1. … g5 2. Qxg5 Be7 and 3. … Bxh4
10) 1. Qb8+ Kf5 2. Qf8+ Kg4 3. Qg8+
11) 1. Qe3 Qb8 2. Re1 (2. … Bxd5 3. Bxd5+ Nf7 4. Rf1)
12) 1. ... Bc5 2. Bxc5 Qxc4+

17   Queen against pawn

AIM OF THE LESSON
- learning more about piece cooperation
- playing according to a plan
- extending the level of endgame skills

PRIOR KNOWLEDGE
- mating with king + queen against king

ACQUISITION

Instruction
In this lesson we focus on endings in which one side has a king and queen and the other side a king and pawn.
In the diagram (⇨) we see a typical position. The pawn has advanced up to the last but one rank, where it is supported by the king. Positions in which the pawn has advanced less far are not of much interest. In such positions the side with the queen wins easily.

In this lesson we will look at a number of winning and drawn positions. By doing this, the students will not only learn to evaluate this type of ending. They will also learn the importance of piece cooperation and planning. It is obvious that these skills are also relevant in other positions.

Simple wins
Before discussing the first diagram, we will discuss some general characteristics of this ending. The diagram (⇩) contains two simple exercises. First, the side with the queen has an easy win if the queen manages to occupy the promotion square. Then all that needs to be done is to bring in the king and take the pawn.

The defending side must try to keep the queen away from the promotion square at all cost.

Weapons of the side with the queen
For now, all the side with the queen must try, is to occupy the promotion square. In the diagram (⇧) there are three possibilities:
- checking the king
- pinning the pawn
- attacking the unprotected pawn (and controlling the promotion square at the same time)

Preventing promotion does not guarantee winning the pawn. It is essential that the side with the queen bring in the king. This can be done only if the pawn is prevented from promotion, either because the pawn is pinned or because the king is positioned on the promotion square. In the left part of the diagram (⇨) the black king must go to the square directly in front of the pawn, otherwise the pawn is lost. After **1. ... Kb1** the threat of promotion has gone, at least until the next move.

The right part of the diagram shows how the previous position can be reached. White attacks the pawn with **1. Qe3**, forcing Black to protect it with **1. ... Kf1**. After **2. Qf3+** Black has to position his king in front of the pawn. That is the moment for the white king to draw a step closer. Now it is time to return to the first diagram (⇩) of this lesson. We will look at a possible continuation (it is important to keep pointing out the parallels with the position in the diagram ⇨).
1. Qe6+ Kf2 2. Qd5 (or 2. Qg4) 2. ... Ke2 3. Qe4+ Kf2 4. Qd3+ Ke1 5. Qe3+ Kd1 and now White can bring his king closer to the pawn; **6. Kd6 Kc2 7. Qe4+ (or 7. Qe2) 7. ... Kc1 8. Qc4+ Kb2 9. Qd3 Kc1 10. Qc3+ Kd1 11. Kd5 Ke2 12. Qc2 Ke1 13. Qe4+ Kf2 14. Qd3 Ke1 15. Qe3+ Kd1 16. Kd4 Kc2 17. Qc3+ Kd1 18. Ke3 Ke1 19. Qxd2+ Kf1 20. Qf2#.**

Positions with rook and bishop pawns
A comment is in order regarding a number of special positions. One of these is shown in the diagram (⇧).
White tries to force the king to the square in front of the pawn: **1. Qb3+**. Black responds with the surprising **1. ... Ka1**. He abandons his pawn with good cause, since Black will be stalemated after **2. Qxc2**. Giving check with the queen does not help; White cannot force Black to occupy the c1-square. Hence, White does not have any opportunity to bring in his king. This defensive strategy is possible only with c-pawns and f-pawns. In such cases, the game will end in a draw.

A similar example is shown in the diagram (⇨). After **1. Qb3+** the black king willingly moves into the corner. Again, the white king cannot approach the pawn as Black would once more be stalemated. The side with the queen therefore cannot reach more than a draw against a-pawns and h-pawns. There are, however, a couple of provisos. Rook and bishop pawns draw only if the following conditions are met:
• The king is close to the pawn.
• The queen cannot occupy the promotion square.
• The enemy king is not too close.

The enemy king is nearby
The last point is vital. If the side with the queen has the king close by, the combined force of king and queen can be used to give mate or conquer the pawn.

In the upper part of the diagram (⇩) Black has the king nearby, and this grants him an easy win: **1. ... Kb6 2. c8Q Qa7#**.
In the lower part of the diagram, White wins with **1. Qf3+ Kg1 2. Ke3 h1Q 3. Qf2#**.

In the left part of the diagram (⇧) White plays
1. Kb3, preventing stalemate. **1. ... Kb1** is met
by **2. Qe1#**.
On the right, White wins the f-pawn after **1.
Ke2**. Black is lost, provided that after **1. ... Kh1**
White does not capture on f2 with the queen.
Once again, the side with the queen wins because
the king is close by.

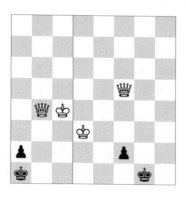

Summary

In ♔+♕ against ♚+♟ endings the side with the
queen almost always wins against b- ,d- ,e- and
g-pawns. If the pawn side has an a- , c- , f- or
h-pawn, the result depends on the position of the
king. The side with the queen has an easy win
if the queen can occupy the promotion square.

PRACTICE

Simultaneous display

Testing the students' skills in this ending can best
be done by having them play game positions to
a finish. A simultaneous display is admirably
suited for this purpose. The trainer plays the
side of the pawns!
In the diagram (⇨) a possible continuation is **1.
Qc4+ Kd2 2. Qb3 Kc1 3. Qc3+ Kb1 4. Kb6
Ka2 5. Qc2 Ka1 6. Qa4+ Kb1 7. Kc5 Kc1
8. Qc4+ Kd2 9. Qb3 Kc1 10. Qc3+ Kb1 11.
Kb4 Ka2 12. Qc2 Ka1 13. Ka3 b1Q 14. Qc3+
Qb2+ 15. Qxb2#.**

In the diagram (⇩) Black can postpone the
impending defeat the longest with **1. Qb5 Kf2
2. Qf5+ Kg2 3. Qe4+ Kf2 4. Qf4+ Kg2 5. Qe3
Kf1 6. Qf3+ Ke1 7. Ke6 Kd2 8. Qf2 Kd1 9.
Qd4+ Kc2 10. Qe3 Kd1 11. Qd3+ Ke1 12. Ke5
Kf2 13. Qd2 Kf1 14. Qf4+ Kg2 15. Qe3 Kf1
16. Qf3+ Ke1 17. Kd4 Kd2 18. Qc3+ Kd1 19.
Kd3 e1Q 20. Qc2#.**

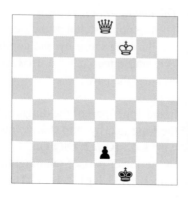

Reminder
◊   *Queen against pawn*

Workbook

☐   *Endgame / Queen against pawn: A*   ♜
Explanation: This exercise sheet contains a combination of winning and drawn positions. The students should find out for themselves whether a given position is winning or drawn. Bright students will discover that all positions in which White is to move are winning and that all positions in which Black is to move are drawn. Noting down the first move is usually sufficient. Ask the students to also indicate the function of the move (see the answers section).
Mistake: The suggested solution is incorrect.
Help: Put the position on a board and play the suggested move. Consider the position from the opponent's perspective. Play the position to a finish if more than one correct move is required.

☐   *Test / Mix: I*   ♜
Explanation: The end of the Step 4 is near. The mixed sheets are a good tool to find out whether the students can apply the topics considered to unfamiliar positions. It is not a good idea to skip these sheets for the sake of convenience. Students who do not obtain a satisfactory result are advised not to continue with Step 5. It is pointless to offer new topics to students who have insufficiently mastered previous topics.
Mistake: The exercise is too difficult.
Help: Ask the student to evaluate the position first, and then offer a specific search strategy.

☐   *Test / Mix: J*   ♜ ♜
Explanation: See Mix: I

ANSWERS

☐   *Endgame / Queen against pawn: A*
1) 1. Qe1 (the queen occupies the promotion square)
2) 1. ... Kc2 (½-½ on account of the rook's pawn; the white king is too far away)

3) 1. Kg3 (1. Qxd2 stalemate)
4) 1. Qa6 (the queen occupies the promotion square)
5) 1. Qe5 Kb3 2. Kf5 c2 3. Qa1 (the queen occupies the promotion

square or the pawn fails to reach the 2nd rank)

6) 1. Kb3 c1Q 2. Qh7+ Ka1 3. Qa7+ (the white king is close enough to the pawn)

7) Drawing

8) Drawing

9) 1. Kd3 (the white king is close enough to the pawn)

10) 1. Kb4 Kb2 2. Ka4+ (the white king is close enough to the pawn)

11) 1. Kf4 f1Q+ 2. Kg3 (the white king is close enough to the pawn)

12) 1. Qb3 or 1. Qa1+ (preventing the black king from occupying the corner)

☐ *Test / Mix: I*

1) 1. Nc7 Qxd6 2. Nxe8+ (double attack: chasing)

2) 1. Ne8 Rdxe8 2. Qf6+ (interfering and square clearing)

3) 1. Bc5 Qxe2 2. Rxe7+

4) 1. Rh8+ Kxh8 2. Bf7# (discovered check: luring)

5) 1. ... Rh2+ 2. Kxh2 Nf3+ (magnet)

6) 1. ... Ra2+ 2. Rd2 Qd7 (placing the front piece)

7) 1. d7 Rd8 2. Qa5 (double attack: chasing)

8) 1. ... Qxb3 2. axb3 Nf3+ (double attack: eliminating the defender)

9) 1. Qh6 gxh6 2. Nxh6# (mate through access)

10) 1. Qd5 Nc6 2. Qxc6 (double attack: luring)

11) 1. Bh6 winning the exchange; 1. ... Re8 2. Bxa6 (attack on the king)

12) 1. Rg7!; 1. Rg8+? Qxg8 2. Bxg8 Rxg8 and Black wins (7th rank)

☐ *Test / Mix: J*

1) 1. ... Nxd5 2. exd5 Qh4+ (double attack: clearing)

2) 1. ... Be5! 2. Qxe5 Nf3+; 2. Qg5 Nf3+ (double attack: luring / chasing)

3) 1. ... Rf1+ 2. Kxf1 Qf5+; 2. Rxf1 Qxe3+ (magnet/luring away + mate)

4) 1. Rh6 gxh6 2. Qf6# (mate through access)

5) 1. ... Qf1+ 2. Rxf1 Rxf1# (mate on account of X-ray protection)

6) 1. Nxc5 Qxc5 2. Qe4 (double attack: clearing)

7) 1. ... Nf3+ 2. Bxf3 Be5# (blocking)

8) 1. Rc8 Qxc8 2. Ne7+ (double attack: luring)

9) 1. Ne7+ Qxe7 2. Qg4+; 1. Qg4+ Kf8 (double attack: clearing / eliminating the defender)

10) 1. ... Re1 2. Qxe1 Qg4#; 2. Re8+ Qxe8+ (luring away + mate)

11) 1. ... Rxe3 2. Qxe3 Bd4

12) 1. Nf6+ Kh8 2. Qg5 with the threat of 3. Qxh6+; 2. ... hxg5 is met by 3. Rh3# (attack on the king: access)

Additional workbooks

As well as the already existing workbooks, Extra workbooks (all Steps), Plus workbooks (Step 1 till 5) and Thinking ahead workbooks (only Step 2 so far) have been published. Many students immediately take on the next step as soon as they have completed a step. Generally speaking, playing strength increases at variable rates. Therefore, the first thing the students should do, is to play more games. The supplementary workbooks allow the students to get more practice at the same level, meaning that they spend more time with the concepts dealt with in a specific step. The important thing is that the degree of difficulty does not rise too quickly. This enables us to some extent to counter any harm that might be done to many students moving on too quickly to the next step and finding that the jump has been too great.

Step 4 extra

A workbook with just a single reminder and apart from that only exercises. The first half of the book contains only exercises on the same themes as those appeared in Step 4 or lower. These are useful not only as additional practice but also particularly so as revision.
In the second half the exercises are all mixed up, and so there is no hint as to the theme of each one. These exercises resemble most closely an actual game. Due to lack of space, there are too few of this type of exercise in the basic workbook which goes with the Step.
Furthermore, repetition is of great significance. Revision is necessary. The reason why we repeat things is not to forget them, so don't forget to repeat.
Subjects from a previous step which are not covered in Step 4 need to be addressed again.

Step 4 plus

In this book there is space for:
• new themes
  – trapping (preparatory moves: luring, eliminating the defence, chasing, targeting and clearing).
  – vulnerability in the opening
  – mini-plan (opening the position)

– solving problems
- themes to which not enough attention was paid in the basic Step because of lack of space
- treatment in more depth of important themes
- themes taken from a previous Step, but at a higher level of difficulty

We deal with all the themes in 11 Plus lessons. Many of these can be short. The main point is that the students are able to solve the exercises in the correct way. We don't advice to skip the instruction.

Playing

In many lessons we need to make room for playing, preferably in the form of a simultaneous display. This advice has been given more than once in previous manuals. Unfortunately we see too often that playing is skipped, partly because the trainer cannot always find appropriate positions, or he hasn't the requisite playing strength or…(?).

When playing positions to a finish we can provide the students with tailor-made material. We can adjust the difficulty to the level of the pupil and give him or her feedback directly. "This was good, but you should avoid attacking when you do not have enough attacking pieces." We improve upon their weaknesses through play. The students find playing fun anyway. The nature of the positions is such that they can often beat the trainer in a simultaneous display. It is important that they realise that their playing strength is increasing all the time. This reinforces their motivation and that in turn is necessary to encourage them to tackle even more energetically their study of chess. This again results in longer term improvements in performance. It is all very simple ….

Julian Hodgson

1⁺   Attacking the king

- learning attacking techniques
- learning to recognise attacking patterns

PRIOR KNOWLEDGE
- attacking the king (lesson 13)

ACQUISITION

Instruction
There are so many (useful) lessons we can give
on attacking the king. In addition to bearing in
mind general rules (bringing up pieces, creating
access, eliminating defenders and delivering
mate) we can deal with typical sacrificial patterns and the coordination of the pieces. In this
lesson we shall take a look at:
- cooperation between the queen and the
  knight
- cooperation between the queen and the
  bishop
- open files
- opening files

Enough material for several training sessions!

Cooperation between queen and knight
In the diagram (⇩) and the following one you
will find a few typical attacking positions, in
which the defender has no hope.
On the left, the rook must move away from c8,
but despite that Black cannot prevent himself
from being mated: **2. Qxa7+ Kc8 3. Qxc7#.**
Only if c7 can be protected again does he have
a chance of escaping mate.
On the right Black is threatening mate in three
ways. The knight's job is to support the mate

with Qg2#. In the other mating patterns (after Nh3# or Ne2#) the queen and knight complement each other.

On the left of the diagram (⇧) Black wins after a rook move with **1. ... Qa2+ 2. Kc1 Qa1+ 3. Kd2 Qxb2+.**
On the right White is threatening mate on h7 and f8. Even if the rook were protected and if Black could play Bf5, White would win with **2. Nh5** and then **3. Qg7#** or **3. Qf6+.**

A queen and a knight move in totally different ways and complement each other particularly well. As we have seen in the first four diagrams they are a perfect match.

Let the students think up a few more typical mating patterns. Knowing and recognising mating patterns is very helpful in finding the correct move.

There is a simple example in the diagram (⇨). White can eliminate the important defending g7-pawn with a sacrifice. He wins by **1. Rxg7+ Rxg7 2. Qxh6+ Kg8 3. Qxg7#.** We recognise the mating pattern from the first diagram.

In this diagram (⇩) Black can still defend after the immediate mating threat with 1. Ng5 Qg7. The knight has to get to f6. White achieves this in a determined manner: **1. Rxf5 gxf5 2. Nf6+.** Black must surrender his queen to prevent mate.

These were known motifs with known mating patterns. It is important to first let the students reflect quietly, so that they are more and more able to turn such positions into the full point in their own games too. The students can mainly solve the examples given in training without too many problems.

A good starting point is to take a look at which mating patterns can be found in a position. In this diagram (⇧) we can redeploy the knight from g5 to f6 or try to chase away the black queen (it is protecting the important point f7), or immediately take on h7. Since the e5-pawn is en prise, 1. Ne4 Qxe5 would make no sense. 1. Qxh7+ Kf8 2. Qh8+ Ng8 would be too hasty, although after 3. h4 White is still better. The correct way is **1. Be4 Qxe5 2. Qxh7+ Kf8 3. Qxf7#**. It is not hard to find if we have first gone through all the options in order. White eliminates the defender, a very useful technique. So we should then ask again what are the various ways to eliminate a defender (taking, chasing away, luring away, interfering and blocking). Examples can be found in the next section.

Cooperation between queen and bishop
The queen and bishop move in the same way, so their cooperation consists mainly of supporting rather than complementing each other. Above all they form an extremely strong attacking weapon when they are on the same diagonal with the queen in front of the bishop. Have the students set up on their own boards a few typical mating patterns with queen and bishop.

In the diagram (⇨) White has to work with a blockade. Without the black bishop on e3 a frequently seen manoeuvre is 1. Qh6 Qxf8 2. Qh7#, and it is one to remember. If the bishop is on e3, White has to go about things differently: **1. Be7! Qxe7 2. Qh7+ Kf8 3. Qh8#**. White has no time for quiet moves: 1. Bb4 Bc5 2. Qh6 Qc7, and White can manage no more than perpetual check.

In this diagram (⇩) too White first has to eliminate a defensive option. Black can still meet an immediate 1. Qf6 with 1. ... e4. So White must first quietly prevent this pawn move with

119

1. e4, after which Qf6 and mate on g7 can no longer be prevented.

In this diagram (⇧), after 1. Qe4 or 1. Qh5 Black can still defend with the move 1. ... f5. So we must prevent this move. After **1. Nf6** Black has to surrender a piece with **1. ... Bg4**. Not a pleasant solution!

As was said, queen and bishop behind each other on the same diagonal constitute a very strong weapon. Such a twofold attack by queen and bishop is often slightly concealed.

In this diagram (⇨) the h7-square is the first target, so White has to eliminate the knight on f6. The move **1. d5** (with the threat 2. Bxf6) is logical. Black has to close the diagonal of the b2-bishop with **1. ... e5**. White now has two good moves, both of which are aimed at increasing the activity of the Bb2:

A) **2. f4 Nd4 3. Bb1** (or **3. fxe5**)

B) **2. Rxe5 Nxe5 3. Bxe5**

In this example the strength of two bishops both of which are aiming at the opposing king is crystal clear.

The final example in which the main roles are played by the queen and the bishop shows how many attacks on the king keep coming back to the same pattern: provoke a weakness and then bring up more pieces. Give the students time to think quietly (diagram ⇩). White hits out with **1. f6 gxf6 2. Qg4+ Kh8 3. Qh4**. This winning method crops up in the Step 4 workbook, but mentioning it just once is not enough.

Open files

In the previous example we already saw that the move d5 opened the diagonal for the Bb2. Pieces which move in straight lines like the rook and bishop should not have pawns blocking their way. We call a file which has none of your own

120

or your opponent's pawns on it an **open file**. In this diagram (⇧), thanks to the open h-file, White has at his disposal a lot of points for his attack. An immediate check does not make sense, since the black king can escape via e6. By playing **1. e6!** White prevents the king's escape for good: **1. ... Bxe6 2. Qh8+ Kf7 3. Rh7#.**

Opening files
If a pawn is getting in the way of a bishop, we move it forward. It is much harder if a pawn is in the way of a rook. There are two ways to get rid of a pawn like that:
• create an opportunity for the pawn to capture something
• force your opponent to capture the pawn

In the left of the diagram (⇨) Black can open the a-file with **1. ... a4**. It makes no difference whether White takes or not.
On the right White has to be careful. After 1. h5 Black prevents the opening of the file with **1. ... g5**. So White needs to start with the preparatory move **1. g5** and only then play **2. h5**. This way of opening a file is an important attacking technique!

A similarly useful technique can be seen in the diagram (⇩). White can achieve nothing on the b-file; Black has enough defenders for the b7-square. The a-file, on the other hand is handed to him on a plate.
After **1. Nb6+ axb6** (or else he loses his queen) **2. axb6+ Kb8** White wins with **3. Ra8+ Kxa8 4. Qa4+.**

On the right White has a choice after **1. ... Ng4**. He can avoid the fatal continuation 2. hxg4 hxg4+ 3. Kg1 Qh2# with **2. g3**. But in the long run, however, White is still on the losing side after **2. ... Qf3+ 3. Kg1 h4**.

The position in this diagram (⇧) is suitable for playing to a finish (simultaneous or against one another). There are no open attacking files. White can try to open the g-file with **1. g4**. Because of the weakening h6 White can open a file with g4-g5 (we could call h6 a point of departure, the weakness serves as a handle). After **1. ... Nxg4 2. Rdg1 h5 3. f3 Ngf6 4. Qh6 Ng4 5. Qxh5** White has the advantage. Black must not take on g4, but after for example **1. ... Nh7 2. f4** White can sooner or later open files on the kingside.

Whenever you discuss the games of your students, keep coming back to the points which were dealt with in this lesson.

PRACTICE

Reminder
◊ *Attacking the king*

Workbook

☐ *Attacking the king / Coordination (♕♘): A*
  Explanation: The queen and knight have a major role to play in the attack, the two pieces bringing about, as it were, a mating pattern. Other attacking pieces have to be sacrificed! In all the positions mate is forced.
  Mistake: The solution is not found.
  Help: Try again. Point out that it is not only the queen and knight which have to move. If needed, demonstrate the mating pattern which is to be achieved.

☐ *Attacking the king / Coordination (♕♗): A*
  Explanation: Queen and bishop cooperate to deliver mate. Sometimes no other help is required, sometimes other pieces have to be sacrificed! Mate is forced in all the positions.
  Mistake: The student cannot find the mate.
  Help: See previous exercise sheet (read 'bishop' for 'knight').

☐ *Attacking the king / Coordination (♕♘): B*
Explanation: See Exercise sheet A. Mate is not forced in all positions. The task has been completed if a considerable gain of material has been achieved.
Mistake: The attack is not decisive.
Help: Set up the position. Have him execute the probable solution and let the student draw his conclusions. It may be that the solution is correct but the student does not think he has gained enough material.

☐ *Attacking the king / Coordination (♕♗): B*
Explanation: Mate is only forced in some of the positions. The squares g7/b7 (g2/b2) are the target. The task has been completed if a considerable gain of material has been achieved.

☐ *Attacking the king / Coordination (♕♗): C*
Explanation: Mate is forced in some positions. The square h7 (h2) is the target. The task has been completed if the mate has been found or if a considerable gain of material has been achieved.

☐ *Attacking the king / Open file: A*
Explanation: The attacking side makes use of the open file to complete the attack successfully (mate or gain of material). The final four positions are demanding.
Mistake: Position 11 is too difficult.
Help: After 1. ... Rg3 2. Kh1 Rxh3+ we have a new task. Have the student solve it (bring up a piece + threaten mate).

☐ *Attacking the king / Opening files: A*
Explanation: One of your own pawns is in the way of a potential attacking piece (the rook). You have to create (or execute) a possible capture for this pawn. Usually the correct way is a sacrifice (with a strong threat).
Mistake: The task is too difficult.
Help: Have the student point out the file which must be opened. How can you get the pawn off that file?

☐ *Attacking the king / Coordination (♕♘): A*

1) 1. Rh8+ Kxh8 2. Qh5+ Kg8 3. Qh7#   Nf3#

2) 1. ... Rh1+ 2. Bxh1 Qh2+ 3. Kf1   8) 1. Nxh6+ gxh6 (1. ... Kh8 2. Nexf7#) Qxf2#   2. Qxf7+ Kh8 3. Ng6#

3) 1. Rxh5 (1. Nf5 f6) 1. ... gxh5 2. Nf5   9) 1. Rd7+ Rxd7 (1. ... Kh8 2. Qxf6+

4) 1. Bxh6+ Kxh6 (1. ... Kh8 2. Qh3)   Kg8 3. Nh6#) 2. Qxf6+ Kg8 3. Nh6#   2. Qh3+ Kg7 3. Qh7#

10) 1. ... Rf1+ 2. Kxf1 Qh1+ 3. Kf2 Ng4#

5) 1. ... Nxe3+ 2. fxe3 (2. Kh1 Nxf2#)   11) 1. ... Rc2 2. Kxc2 Qxa2#   2. ... Qg3+ 3. Kh1 (3. Kf1 Qf2#) 3.   12) 1. Qf6 Qa5 (1. ... Qxe7 2. Qh8#; 1.   ... Nf2#   ... Rxe7 2. Qh8#) 2. Ng6+ Kg8 3.

6) 1. Rh8+ Bxh8 2. Nh6+ Kf8 3. Qf7#   Qh8#

7) 1. ... Qf3+ 2. Kxh2 Qh3+ 3. Kg1

☐ *Attacking the king / Coordination (♕♗): A*

1) 1. ... Bh2+ 2. Kh1 Bg3+ 3. Kg1 Qh2#   8) 1. ... Rg3+ 2. fxg3 Bh3 3. Re2 Qf1#

2) 1. ... Bxg2+ 2. Bxg2 Qh4+ 3. Bh3   9) 1. ... Nxc3+ 2. Bxc3 Qxc3 3. a3 Qa1#   Qxh3#   10) 1. ... Qh4+ 2. Kf1 Bh3+ 3. Kg1 Qd4#

3) 1. Rb8+ Bf8 2. Rxf8+ Kxf8 3. Qc8#   11) 1. ... Rxg2 2. Kxg2 Qh3+ 3. Kh1

4) 1. Rxe7+ Kxe7 2. Qe6+ Kf8 3. Qf7#   Qf3#

5) Drawing   12) 1. Rh8+ Kxh8 2. Qxh6+ Kg8 3.

6) 1. Ng5 h6 2. Qg6 hxg5 3. Qh5#   Qxg7#

7) 1. Rh8+ Bxh8 2. Qg8+ Kh6 3. Qxh8#

☐ *Attacking the king / Coordination (♕♘): B*

1) 1. Nf6 Qxf6 2. Qxf8#   7) 1. Ng5 Bxg5 (1. ... Rg8 2. Qxh7#)

2) 1. Neg5 (or 1. Nfg5) 1. ... fxg5 2.   2. Qg7#   Nxg5   8) 1. Rxh5 gxh5 2. Nxh5

3) 1. Rxh5 (1. Nf5 Nf8) 1. ... gxh5 2.   9) 1. Ba3 Bxa3 2. Ng5 (of 2. Nf6+)   Nf5   10) 1. Ng5 Qe8 2. Nxe6+ Kg8 3. Qxg7#

4) 1. Nh5 gxh5 2. Nf6+   11) 1. Rxh7+ Bxh7 2. Qh5

5) 1. Ngf5 exf5 2. Nxf5   12) 1. Ne4 Bxg5 2. Nxg5

6) 1. Nh5 Bf8 2. Nf6+ Kh8 3. Qxh7#

☐ *Attacking the king / Coordination (♕♗): B*

1) 1. Re8+ Bf8 (1. ... Qxe8 2. Qg5+   5) 1. Qc6 (1. Ba6 Qe4) 1. ... f4 2. Ba6   Ng7 3. Qxg7#) 2. Rxd8   Qc8 3. Bxc8

2) 1. Qg5+ Ng6 2. Qh6   6) 1. Rf1 (1. Bxe7 f6 ; 1. Qh6 Nf5) 1.

3) 1. Bf4 Nd7 2. Rxd7 Qxd7 3. Bh6   ... Qd7 2. Qh6

4) 1. ... Be5 2. Rd1 Qf3   7) 1. Nh5+ gxh5 2. Qg5+

8) 1. g4 Nc6 2. Qf6
9) 1. f5 (1. Qh6 Nf5) 1. ... Qe8 2. Qh6
10) 1. Bf6 Rc7 2. Qh6

11) 1. Bf4 (1. Bh6 Qc3) 1. ... Qc3 2. Be5
12) 1. ... Nxe4 2. Nxe4 (2. Bxe4 Bxc3)
    2. ... Qa3+ 3. Kb1 Qb2#

Attacking the king / Coordination (♕♗): C

1) 1. Rh5 gxh5 2. Qxh7#
2) 1. Qg4+ Kh8 2. Qf5 (2. Qh5 f5 3. Bxf5 f6)
3) 1. Rh8+ (1. Qh5 f5) 1. ... Kxh8 2. Qh5+ Kg8 3. Qh7#
4) 1. Bxf6+ Bxf6 2. Qe4
5) 1. Nf6 Bxf6 2. Bd3
6) 1. Bxf6 (1. Rxe7 Qxe7 2. Ne4 Ne5) 1. ... Bxf6 2. Qf5
7) 1. Qg4+ Kh8 2. Qf5

8) 1. ... Rxg2+ 2. Bxg2 Bh2+ 3. Kh1 Bg3+
9) 1. ... Rxh3+ 2. gxh3 (2. Qxh3 Qxd1#) 2. ... Qh2#
10) 1. Ng6+ fxg6 2. Qxg6
11) 1. ... Nxe4 2. Nxe4 Qxa2+ 3. Kc1 Qa1#
12) 1. Bg7 (1. Bg5 Re8 ; 1. Bf4 Re8) 1. ... h6 2. Qxh6 Bxg7 3. Qh7#

Attacking the king / Open file: A

1) 1. Qf6+ Bxf6 2. Rg3+
2) 1. Qh6 (1. Qh5 Rff8) 1. ... Rff8 2. Qxg7#
3) 1. Rh7+ Kxh7 2. Qxf7+ Kh8 3. Rh1+
4) 1. ... Qxc3 2. bxc3 Ne4
5) 1. Qf6+ Bxf6 2. gxf6+ Kg8 3. Rxh8#
6) 1. ... Bxa2+ 2. Nxa2 Qa5
7) Drawing
8) 1. Bf7 Qxh4 (1. ... c2 2. Rg8+ Rxg8 3. Rxg8# ; 1. ... Qxf7 2. Qxd8+) 2.

Rg8+ Rxg8 3. Rxg8#
9) 1. Rh5 Rg6 (1. ... Rg8 2. Qxg8+ Qxg8 3. Rxg8+ Kxg8 4. Rxh6 ; 1. ... Rf7 2. Qg8#) 2. Qxg6
10) Drawing
11) 1. ... Rg3 2. Kh1 Rxh3+ 3. Rh2 Qg6! 4. Qf2 Rxh2+ 5. Qxh2 Be4+.
12) 1. f6 Bxg2 (1. ... Qxf6 2. Qxb4+) 2. Rg8+ Kxg8 3. Qxg2+

Attacking the king / Opening files: A

1) 1. ... Nf3+ 2. gxf3 (2. Kh1 Nxd2) 2. ... gxf3+ 3. Kh1 Qg2#
2) 1. Ng5 Bxg5 2. hxg5+ Kg8 3. Qh7+ Kf8 4. Qh8#
3) 1. Ng5 fxg5 2. hxg5
4) 1. g5 gxh5 2. gxh6
5) 1. Qb6+ cxb6 (1. ... Ka8 2. Qxc5) 2. axb6#
6) 1. ... Bg4 2. Nxg4 hxg4 and wins, e.g. 3. Qc3 Bh2+ 4. Kh1 Bg3+ 5.

Kg1 Rh1+ 6. Kxh1 Qh5+ 7. Kg1 Qh2#
7) 1. Rxh5 gxh5 2. g6
8) 1. Nf5 exf5 2. gxf5+ Kh8 3. Qg2
9) 1. Nxg5+ hxg5 2. h6 Rg8 3. hxg7+
10) 1. ... Qg3 2. hxg4 hxg4
11) 1. Qh6+ Bxf6 (1. ... gxh6 2. gxh6#) 2. gxf6
12) 1. Rg4 g5 2. Rxg5

2⁺ Vulnerability in the opening

AIM OF THE LESSON
• learning how to exploit vulnerability in the opening

PRIOR KNOWLEDGE
• all forms of combinations

ACQUISITION

Instruction
In the workbook three motifs concerning vulnerability in the opening are dealt with: Legal's mate (reminder and exercise pages), the e8-h5 diagonal and the e-file (both only exercise pages).

The reminder 'Legal's mate' contains enough examples. The e-file was dealt with in lesson 5⁺ of Step 3. In this lesson we shall treat only the third motif.

A vulnerable diagonal
The h5-e8 (or h4-e1) diagonal is vulnerable (just think of the quickest possible mate: **1. f3 e5 2. g4 Qh4#**). As soon as the f-pawn disappears, a check on h4-h5 is often annoying, since usually the only piece which can interposed is the g-pawn.
Unsuspecting players of the white pieces in the King's Gambit frequently capture too soon on e5. After **1. e4 e5 2. f4 Nc6 3. fxe5? Qh4+** we get the position in the diagram (⇩). White loses immediately. After **4. g3 Qxe4+ 5. Qe2 Qxh1 6. Nf3 Bc5** White is simply a rook down and cannot trap the queen. And **4. Ke2 Qxe4+ 5. Kf2 Bc5+ 6. d4 Bxd4+ 7. Kg3 Nge7** is not much fun either.

The f-pawn can be diverted or lured away in various ways. In this diagram (⇧) White plays **1. Nxe6** and wins at least a pawn: **1. ... fxe6 2. Qh5+ g6 3. Bxg6+** and Black cannot survive. After **1. ... Qc8 2. Nb5** or **1. ... Qe7 2. Nxd5** Black remains in difficulties.

The weakening h7-h6
In the game Krogius–Ojanen, Helsinki 1951, the disadvantages of the weakening of h6 soon become apparent. We should let the students analyse the important moments in pairs.
1. e4 c5 2. d4 cxd4 3. Nf3 e5
Ask what the best move is. It is the move in the game and not 4. Nxe5 Qa5+.
4. c3 dxc3 5. Nxc3 d6 6. Bc4 h6 (see the diagram ⇨).
Black wants to play Nf6 without allowing Ng5. Simply continuing with his development gives White sufficient compensation. 7. Qb3 is strong, but White cannot take advantage of the weakening of the e8-h5 diagonal. The students often find the winning move.
7. Bxf7+ Kxf7 8. Nxe5+ Ke7
Let us follow the game.
Other moves are:

A) **8. ... Ke8 9. Qh5+ Ke7 10. Qf7#**
B) **8. ... Ke6 9. Qd5+ Kf6 10. Qf7+ Kxe5 11. Bf4+ Kd4 12. Qd5#**
C) **8. ... Kf6** (see the diagram ⇩).
White has two strong moves.
   C1) 9. Qf3+ Kxe5 10. Qf7 Nf6 11. f4+ Kd4 12. Ne2+ (or even 12. Be3+ Kxe3 13. 0-0-0 Bg4 14. Rhe1+ Kxf4 15. g3+ Ke5 16. Rd5+ Nxd5 17. exd5+ Kd4 18. Re4+ Kd3 19. Qf1+) 12. ... Kxe4 13. Ng3+ Kd4 14. Be3+ Kxe3 15. Qc4 followed by mate.
   C2) 9. Qd4 (a deadly battery) 9. ... Qe8 10. Nd5+ or 9. ... Ke6 10. Qd5+ Kf6 11. Qf7+ Kxe5 12. Bf4+ Kd4 13. Qd5#
9. Nd5+ Ke6 10. Qg4+ Kxe5 11. Bf4+

(see the diagram ⇧)

11. ... Kd4

Or 11. ... Kxe4 12. Nc3+ Kd4 (12. ... Kd3 13. 0-0-0+ Kc4 14. Qe2+ Kc5 15. Qb5#) 13. Be3++ Ke5 14. Bd4#

12. Be3+ Ke5 13. Qf4+ Ke6 14. Qf5#

A game which always goes down well.

For those who are looking for more sample games, there are some beautiful games in From's Gambit (**1. f4 e5 2. fxe5 d6 3. exd6 Bxd6**).

PRACTICE

Reminder

◊ *Opening: Legal's mate*

Workbook

☐ *Vulnerability in the opening / The h5/e8 diagonal: A*
Explanation: In all the positions White can take advantage of the h5/e8 diagonal (h4/e1 for Black) . The diagonal is already open or can be opened. The defending side can usually prevent the mate but has to lose material to do so.

☐ *Vulnerability in the opening / Discovered attack: A*
Explanation: This is an unusual worksheet in the sense that the first move is already known: 1. Nxe5. White breaks the pin on his knight. The idea behind the exercise is that the students get to know the various continuations which can arise after the sacrifice of the queen.

☐ *Vulnerability in the opening / Discovered attack (yes or no): B*
Explanation: Is 1. Nxe5 right or wrong? Is there or is there not a discovered attack. The students must give a reason (see the answers).
Mistake: The answer is wrong.
Help: Check the solution proposed. Where can the opponent play a better move?

☐ *Vulnerability in the opening / The e-file: A*
Explanation: This subject was dealt with in detail in Lesson 5[+] of Step 3. This worksheet constitutes good revision at a higher level. In all the

positions White can win material with some operation in which the e-file has an important role to play.

☐ *Vulnerability in the opening / The h5-e8 diagonal: A*

1) 1. e6 fxe6 2. Qh5+
2) 1. Be2
3) 1. Ne5 fxe5 2. Qh5+ g6 3. Qxg6#
4) 1. Nd6+ exd6 2. Qh5#
5) 1. ... Ne3 2. fxe3 Bh4+ 3. Nxh4 Qxh4+ 4. g3 Qxg3#
6) 1. Nf6+ gxf6 2. Qh5+ (2. exf6+ also wins) 2. ... Ke7 3. Qf7#
7) 1. Rxe6+ fxe6 2. Qh5#

8) 1. Ne6 hxg5 (1. ... fxe6 2. Qh5+)
2. Nxd8
9) 1. Bh5+ g6 (1. ... Ke7 2. Ba3#) 2. Nxg6 hxg6 3. Bxg6+ Ke7 4. Ba3#
10) 1. Nxe6 fxe6 2. Bh5+ Ke7 3. Qxd6#
11) 1. Ne5 fxe5 2. Qh5+ Kf8 3. Qf7#
12) 1. ... Ng3 2. Rh2 Nxe2

☐ *Vulnerability in the opening / Discovered attack: A*

1) 1. Nxe5 Bxd1 2. Bb5+ Qd7 3. Bxd7+
2) 1. Nxe5 Bxd1 2. Bxf7#
3) Drawing
4) 1. Nxe5 Bxd1 (1. ... dxe5 2. Qxg4) 2. Bxf7+ Ke7 3. Bg5#
5) 1. Nxe5 Bxd1 2. Bxd7+ Qxd7 3. Nxd7 Bxc2 4. Nxf8 winning a piece.
6) 1. Nxe5 Qxe5 (1. ... fxe5 2. Qxg4; 1. ... Bxd1 2. Nxc6+ Ne7 3. Nxa5) 2. Rxe5+ Nxe5 3. Be2

7) 1. Nxe5 Bxd1 2. Bxf7+ Ke7 3. Nf5#
8) 1. Nxe5 Bxe2 (1. ... Nxe5 2. Qxh5+) 2. Bf7+ Kf8 3. Bh6#
9) 1. Nxe5 Nxe5 (1. ... Bxd1 2. Nxc6+) 2. Qxg4 0-0 3. Qd1
10) 1. Nxe5 Bxd1 2. Bb5+ Kd8 3. Nxf7+
11) 1. ... Nxe4 2. Bxe7 Bxf2+ 3. Kf1 Ng3#
12) 1. Nxe5 Bxd1 2. Neg6+ (2. Ne6+ Ke7 3. Nxd8) 2. ... fxg6 3. Nxg6#

☐ *Vulnerability in the opening / Discovered attack (yes / no): B*

1) No: 1. Nxe5? Bxd1 2. Bxf7+ Ke7 3. Bg5+ Nf6. For it to be mate a knight is needed on c3.
2) No: 1. Nxe5? Bxd1 2. Bxf7+ Kf8. The f8-square is free for the king.
3) Yes: 1. Nxe5 Bxd1 2. Bxf7+ Ke7 3. Bg5#
4) No: 1. Nxe5? Nxe5, and the bishop on g4 is protected; (1. ...

Bxd1? 2. Bxf7+ Ke7 3. Nd5#)
5) Yes: 1. Nxe5 Bxd1 2. Bxf7+ Ke7 3. Nd5#
6) Yes: 1. Nxe5 Bxd1 (1. ... dxe5 2. Qxg4 Nxc2) 2. Bf7+ Ke7 3. Nd5#
7) No: 1. Nxe5? Nxb3! 2. Nxg4 Nxa1; 1. ... Bxd1? 2. Bxf7+ Ke7 3. Nd5#
8) No: 1. Nxe5? Bxd1 2. Bxf7+ Ke7.

The move 3. Nd5+ is not possible.
9) Yes: 1. Nxe5 Bxd1 2. Nf6+ gxf6
3. Bxf7#
10) No: 1. Nxe5? Bxd1 2. Bxf7+ Ke7
3. Nd5#

11) Yes: 1. Nxe5 Bxd1 2. Nf6+ gxf6
3. Bxf7#
12) Yes: 1. Nxe5 Bxd1 2. Bxf7+ Ke7
3. Nd5#; 1. ... dxe5 (the best) 2.
Qb3 with advantage.

☐ *Vulnerability in the opening / The e-file: A*
1) 1. e5 Qxe5 2. Re1
2) 1. Nxe5 fxe5 (1. ... Bxd1 2.
Nxc6+) 2. Qxg4
3) 1. Qxf5 exf5 2. Nxc6+
4) 1. Nd6+ Bxd6 2. Qxf5
5) 1. Nc4 Qc7 2. Nd6+
6) 1. Nf6+ gxf6 2. Qxd5
7) 1. Nf6+ gxf6 2. Qxd5
8) 1. Nxe4 Qxd4 (1. ... dxe4 2.

Qxe4+) 2. Nf6+ Kd8 3. Re8#.
9) 1. Qxd5 exd5 2. exd6+
10) 1. Nd6+ Kd7 (1. ... exd6 2. exd6+)
2. Nxf7
11) 1. Nxf7 Nc6 2. Qh4 Bxf7 3.
Rxe7+
12) 1. Nd5 Qb7 2. Nc7+ Kd8 3.
Rxd7+

130

3⁺ Interference

Interference

AIM OF THE LESSON
• deepening knowledge of the concept 'interference'

PRIOR KNOWLEDGE
• interference (lesson 2)

ACQUISITION

Instruction
Interference was already discussed in lesson 2 of the basic part of Step 4. With the help of the diagram (⇨) we check how much has been retained. The important defender is the rook on b3. It is protecting the weak point f3. Swapping off the rook with 1. ... Rc3 is not good enough; White plays 2. f4. The rook move is not forcing enough. The way to win is by interfering with the link between the rook and f3 **1. ... Bc3**. Once more, f3 is en prise, but at the same time there is the threat of **2. ... Bxb4**.
If it is required, deal with other forms of interference from the second lesson. In this lesson we shall treat interference with the help of chasing and luring. In addition the simultaneous interference with two pieces is dealt with.

Chasing
A quite simple but very effective form is shown in the diagram (⇩). The black rooks are protecting one another, and at first sight everything appears to be just fine. However, a check on b8 changes the situation drastically. The king has to move on to the same rank as the rook, meaning that suddenly the rook on a7 is unprotected: **1. Qb8+ Kd7 2. Qxa7+**. It is worth noting that the queen goes hunting all alone, creates the

interference and scoops up the booty.

In the lower part we see a similar picture. Black plays **1. … Qh1+**, and once again the king has to interfere with the way a rook is offering protection, this time the rook on e1.

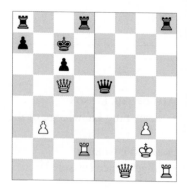

It is remarkable how often this interference brought about by the queen is to be found in practical play. In this diagram (⇧) the opposing king has more options, so that the queen requires help. On the left the white queen gives check: **1. Qa5+**. If Black plays **1. … Kb7**, then all that is needed is **2. Rxd8**. But in this position the king can continue to protect its rook on d8 with **1. … Kc8**, but the twofold attack on d8 means that a rook is lost here too.

In the position on the right White cannot be saved after **1. … Qe4+**. None of the three legal moves offers a way out: **2. Kf2 Rxh1**; **2. Kg1 Rxh1+** or **2. Qf3 Qxf3+ 3. Kxf3 Rxh1**.

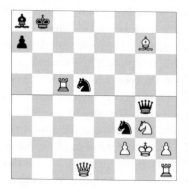

In this diagram (⇨) the attacking side needs the help of another piece so as to be able to catch his prey. In the top half White gives a check with **1. Be5+**. Black's only option is to move his king on to the diagonal of his bishop. After **1. … Kb7** White wins a piece with **2. Rxd5**.

In the bottom half Black plays **1. … Nh4+** and chases the white king on to the back rank. After **2. Kg1 Qxd1+** a whole queen is the booty.

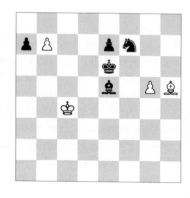

In the examples which have been dealt with, the defender has been protecting another piece. The function of the defender can also be the protection of a square. In the diagram (⇩) the b-pawn is just about to promote. But for the moment the bishop is still preventing that promotion. With **1. Bg4+ Kd6 2. b8Q**.

White chases the king on to d6, after which he can get a queen.

Luring

When a piece is being chased it has no choice, when it is being lured it does: the defending side can choose which way to be defeated. Another example with passed pawns. In the diagram (⇧) after **1. e7** Black has to battle against two far advanced passed pawns. He has the choice between:

A) **1. ... Bc6**, after which White wins by diverting the defender: **2. e8Q Bxe8 3. a8Q**.

B) **1. ... Re4**, after which we have the subject of this lesson. White promotes with **2. a8Q**

A clever check lets us eliminate a defender by means of interference. In this diagram (⇨) we have bits from the opening phase of the game. In the upper half a queen is enough to create havoc on its own. After **1. Qc6+** Black has two ways of getting out of check. After. **1. ... Nd7 2. Qxd5** the link between the defending queen and the d5-knight is blocked, and after **1. ... Qd7 2. Qxa8+** the protection of the rook on a8 has been removed.

In the bottom half **1. ... Bd3+** is a deadly check. White cannot take the bishop: **2. Qxd3 Qf2+**, but if he interposes a knight there follows **2. ... Qf2#**.

In this diagram (⇩) White is far behind in material. His only chance consists of taking advantage of the bad position of the black king. Because the king is hemmed in White can give perpetual check with 1. Nf2+ Kg1 2. Nh3+, but there is more in the position for him. After **1. Kf3** there is the threat of mate with **2. Bg2#**. Black is forced to give check with **1. ... Nd4+** (1. ... Ne5+ 2. Kg3). After **2. Kf2** mate cannot be avoided. White must first lure the black knight on to d4, to prevent a queen check. After the over-hasty 1. Kf2 Black wins with 1. ... Qb6+.

Interfering with the action of two pieces
So far we have always eliminated only one piece by interfering with its line of action. We shall now take a look at positions in which we can interfere with the working of two pieces which move in straight lines at the same time. In this diagram (⇧) White cannot get a queen straight away. After 1. e8Q Bxe8 2. Rxe8 Rxg7 White does not have a big enough advantage. So to get some benefit from his two passed pawns White must look for a square where the lines of the two defending pieces meet and cross over. The g6-square is that intersection point. So with the beautiful move **1. Rg6** White can eliminate one of the defenders (in fact both defenders!). **1. ... Bxg6** is followed by **2. g8Q**, and after **1. ... Rxg6** it is the e-pawn which promotes.

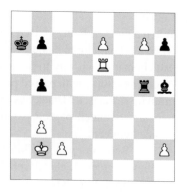

In the diagram (⇨) the black rooks are preventing White from mating with a knight check. The intersection point for the rooks is f6. Bearing in mind the previous example, **1. Bf6+** comes as no real surprise. It does not matter how Black captures:
After **1. ... Rexf6** (after 1. ... gxf6 White can deliver mate in three ways) the rook on f6 suddenly has two jobs: preventing mate on f3 and also on g6. Diverting it decides: **2. Nf3+** (and not 2. Ng6+ Rxg6 when the Rf8 is still controlling f3) **2. ... Rxf3 3. Ng6#**.
The variation for the other rook: **1. ... Rfxf6 2. Ng6+ Rxg6 3. Nf3#**.

In the diagram (⇩) you can see the final example for this lesson. Let the students puzzle it out for a bit. Where can White deliver mate? On f2, if there were no rook on a2, and on d4, if there were no bishop on a1. White mates in two with **1. Rb2!**

134

Reminder
◊ *Blocking and interfering*

Workbook

☐ *Eliminating of the defence / Interfering: A*
Explanation: First of all we must look for important defenders. Interfering (with a lot of "chasing" and sometimes "attracting") allows us to eliminate defenders. They do need to get used to this, but whenever the students have got the knack of it, they can easily solve the exercises.
Mistake: The student cannot manage the tasks.
Help: Does the student understand what the exercise is all about? Ask what he has already tried. Let the student speak about it and give some help where it is needed. The tasks are really not difficult.

☐ *Eliminating of the defence / Interfering: B*
Explanation: This page contains only tasks where two defenders have to be eliminated. The side which is in a superior position would like to deliver mate or promote a passed pawn. Eliminating one or two defenders allows this wish to be fulfilled.
Mistake: The student cannot manage the tasks.
Help: What do you want to do? According to the task, the answer is 'mate' or 'promote a pawn'. Look for the intersection point of the two defending pieces. Can you lure a piece on to it?

☐ *Eliminating of the defence / Interfering: A*
1) 1. Ba4+ Nd7 2. Nd6#
2) 1. ... Qh1+ 2. Ke2 Qxg2+
3) 1. ... Qg2+ 2. Ke1 Qxh1+
4) 1. Qg5+ Kf8 2. Qxd8+
5) 1. e5 Ne8 (1. ... Rae8 2. exf6) 2. Qxa8
6) 1. Qf3+ Kg8 2. Qxa8+

7) 1. ... Ba6+ 2. Nge2 Qf2#
8) 1. c5 Be7 2. Bxe6+
9) 1. ... Qg6+ 2. Kf1 Qxb1+
10) 1. h3 Ne5 2. Bxf4
11) 1. a5 Nd7 2. Bxf5
12) 1. ... g5 2. Ne2 Nxe4

1) 1. Be4 Rxe4 (1. ... Bxe4 2. Ne6#)
2. Ng6#

2) 1. Ne6 Rxe6 (1. ... Bxe6 2. e8Q+)
2. c8Q Rxe7 3. Qc5+

3) 1. e7 Bxe7 (1. ... Rd6 2. exd8Q+
Rxd8 3. Nf6#) 2. Ng7#

4) 1. ... Nf3 2. Bxf3 (2. R4xf3 Qg2#)
2. ... Qxf1#

5) 1. Bc6 Bxc6 (1. ... Rxc6 2. Nf3#)
2. Ng6#

6) 1. Nb2 Rxb2 (1. ... Bxb2 2. b8Q)
2. g7

7) 1. Nb7 Bxb7 (1. ... Rxb7 2. c8Q#)
2. cxb8Q+

8) 1. Be4 Bxe4 (1. ... Rxe4 2. Nd5#;
1. ... Qd4 2. Qe1#) 2. Ng4#

9) 1. Bd3 Rdxd3 (1. ... Rcxd3 2.
d8Q+ Rxd8 3. Rh1+ Rh2 4.
Rxh2#) 2. Rh1+ Rh3 3. d8Q+

10) 1. Nfe4 Bxe4 (1. ... Rxe4 2. Nf5#;
1. ... b2 2. Bc3#) 2. Ne2#

11) 1. e4 Rf4 (1. ... Rxe4 2. Nf3#; 1. ...
Bxe4 2. Nc4#) 2. Re6#

12) 1. ... Bc3 2. Bxc3 Rxc6

AIM OF THE LESSON
- going more deeply into the concept of blocking

PRIOR KNOWLEDGE
- blocking (lesson 4)

ACQUISITION

Instruction

Blocking was dealt with in lesson 4 of the basic part of Step 4. In the first two positions we roughly revise what has already been discussed. In the diagram (⇨) White is short of attacking pieces of his own and must make use of blocking. With some clever checks his queen makes sure that the black pieces all have to move on to the important escape squares for the king: **1. Qd8+ Be8 2. Qd6+ Qe7 3. Qh6#.**

In this diagram (⇩) a check with the bishop is not sufficient. After 1. Bf3+ Black has 1. ... Bd5 (on account of 2. d5 king moves are out of the question), 1. ... Kb5 and 1. ... Kd7, and after 1. Be8+ the move 1. ... Kd5 is the correct choice (1. ... Bd7 2. d5+). With **1. d5+** White eliminates these defensive options. The pawn sacrifice is a multi-faceted move. First of all there is the double attack, forcing Black to capture. After **1. ... Kxd5 2. Bf3+** the pawn move acts as a magnet, and after **1. ... Bxd5 2. Be8+** the blocking motif becomes clear.

The most important thing the two positions (and all the positions from lesson 4) have in common is the 'check'. This means that the course of play is more or less forced.

Let us turn to positions without check but where there is still a blocking motif. How can we deprive the opposing king of a square by blocking? We deal with three ways:

- **luring (attracting)**
- **chasing**
- **zugzwang**

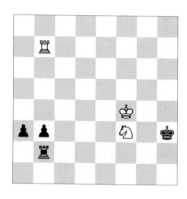

We must oblige our opponent to move a piece to the fatal square. Threats are very good for that purpose.

Luring by threatening mate
Above, in the diagram (⇧) the attacking side works with a threat of mate to entice the defender on to the fatal square.
White plays **1. Rg7** (threatening mate on g3) **1. ... Rg2** (the only way to prevent 2. Rg3#) **2. Rh7#**.

In the diagram (⇨) we exclude the move 1. Nxa2 stalemate. The position of the black king is just crying out for a mate. White can deliver mate with the knight on c7. How does the knight get there? Via b5 or d5 – or does it matter? Only **1. Nd5 Ra7** (only move) **2. Nb6#** wins. The rook is now blocking its own king. After 1. Nb5? Black can still save himself with 1. ... Ra7. After any capture Black is stalemated.

In the diagram (⇩) the threat after **1. Ne4** is mate with 2. Nf6#. The defence **1. ... Bc3** (hoping for 2. Nxc3 Bf5) fails to **2. Ng3#**. The other possibility to take control of f6 is **1. ... Bxh4**, but then the knight on g6 no longer has to protect the h4-pawn, so **2. Nf4#** decides matters.

Luring by threatening promotion
A pawn which is approaching the opponent's back rank is extremely dangerous. The threatened promotion usually forces the opponent to

sacrifice material for the pawn. In the examples which are dealt with, he does not get off so lightly.

In this diagram (⇧) White can win a piece with **1. Bb2+ Ke7 2. Nc6+ Kxe6 3. Nxa5**, but without a white pawn the win is not possible. We can make better use of the passed pawn as follows: **1. e7** (the ultimate sacrifice to force mate). Then **1. … Nxe7** is forced and the black king has no escape squares left and it is all over with it after **2. Bb2#**. Now the white pawn is no longer needed.

In this diagram (⇨) too the black king is wretchedly placed. The position of the king and bishop tempts White to play 1. Nd6 (threatening mate) 1. … Kg7? 2. Nf5+ winning. Of course Black must play 1. … hxg6. The passed pawn must once more be sacrificed in order to make victory possible: **1. g7+ Bxg7 2. Nd6**, and the bishop on g7 blocks the king. Black is able to move the bishop away, but misfortune has already befallen him: **2. Nf5#** is nevertheless mate.

A third example is portrayed in the diagram (⇩). Both sides have a dangerous passed pawn. But here too the worse position of the black king is the deciding factor (and the fact is White is to move!). However White achieves nothing with a direct attack: 1. Bc5+ Ka6 (1. … Ka8? 2. Rb8#) 2. Rb6+ Ka5 3. c7 Ba6+ 4. Kb8 Rg8+, and Black has the queening square sufficiently under his control.

In order to win White must liquidate to a bishop ending, although it looks as though he would immediately lose the passed pawn: **1. Rb7+ Rxb7 2. cxb7 Ba6**. The only move which prevents the promotion of the b-pawn. Now the black king no longer has any freedom of movement and White can bring matters to a conclusion with **2. Bc5#**.

Luring by threatening to win material
The first example shows this intention best of all. In the left of the diagram (⇧) White is threatening to win the black knight with a check on (chasing away + material). Black is powerless against this threat. The only 'safe' square for the knight leads to a mate because the king's escape is blocked: **1. ... Nd8 2. Nb6#.**

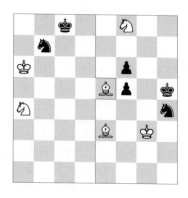

On the right White plays **1. Ne6** and threatens to win the black knight with **2. Nf4+ Kg5 3. Ng2+.** Black does not have many moves. **1. ... f4+** makes no sense: **2. Nxf4+ Kg5 3. Ng2+.** A king move gives up the protection of the knight. The knight is lost after every move by Black except **1. ... Ng6**, but that move is followed by **2. Ng7#.**

Chasing
By attacking a piece we chase it on to the square we want to see it on.
On the left in the diagram (⇨) Black chases the knight away with **1. ... Kb2.** The desired result is **2. Nb4 Nc3#.** It is worth taking a look at another white counter-attack: **2. Kb5 Kxa2 3. Kc6 Ka3 4. Kxd5 b5**, and Black wins.

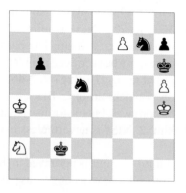

On the right White must be careful. Promoting the f-pawn to a queen leads to stalemate, and not promoting is no good either on account of 1. ... Ne6. So the correct move is **1. f8R**, which threatens mate on f6. The knight does not have many moves; it is an immediate loss after **1. ... Ne6 2. Rf6+**, but even **1. ... Nxh5 2. Rf5** does not last long. The only 'safe' square is g7, but there it blocks the king: **2. ... Ng7 3. Rf6#.**

In this diagram (⇩) the final white pawn is under threat of being lost. So White plays **1. Rh6.** The knight must move away. 1. ... Nf8 2. g6 does not achieve anything. Thinking of the subject of this lesson we play **1. ... Nxg5 2. Rh4#.**

Two other examples with chasing can be seen in the diagram (⇧).

At the top, White can take advantage of the restricted freedom of movement of the black rook. After **1. Kg6!** The rook cannot go to h8 because of the X-ray check on a8. The other safe square is d7, but if it goes there then White plays **2. Ra8#**.

In the bottom half the final white pawn seems about to fall. White can keep it alive with a clever manoeuvre: **1. Ne2!** White gains time to be able to protect the pawn by 2. g3. The technique required to win after **1. ... Rg8 2. g3** is not so difficult. For the sake of completeness: **1. ... Rxg2** is followed by **2. Rh4#**.

Zugzwang
In this diagram (⇨) White cannot take the black queen on account of stalemate. After the strong **1. Rb1** Black is in zugzwang. He would love to miss a move since White does not have any useful moves either. The move e3-e4 would give the black king the d4-square. 'Passing' is of course not allowed, so the queen must move to the only square on which it cannot be taken: **1. ... Qd2 2. Rb3#**.

A final form of blocking is when one side blocks itself 'voluntarily', by mistake. You always have to be on your guard whenever your own king has limited freedom of movement.
In this diagram (⇨) White has a great advantage. There is not much Black can do (above all his bishop on c8 is a cause of worry). It is tempting for White to play **1. Be4** and immediately have a go at the h7-pawn which is hard to defend. The bishop move deprives its own king of the e4-square, which is immediately decisive after **1. ... b5!**. The white king can no longer go to

c4, and the threat of **2. ... Bb7#** can also not be delayed for any length of time.

Reminder
◊ *Blocking and interfering*

Workbook

☐ *Eliminating the defender / Blocking: A*
   Explanation: With the correct move, the side whose move it is can either "chase" or "lure" an opposing piece on to a fatal square. It will be fatal because that piece will get in the way of its own king, leading to the latter being mated. An easy practice sheet with some more demanding tasks.

Mistake: Position 5 is too difficult.

Help: The first move of the solution does not directly attack anything, but after 1. Nd6 there is the threat of: 2. Nc4+ Kb5 3. Nb2+. Get the student to point out all of Black's possible moves. A move by the king loses a knight, the pawn move 1. ... c4 would be possible, as would 1. ... Nb6. How can White prevent both possibilities?

☐ *Eliminating the defence / Blocking: A*
1) 1. Rg6 Nf5 2. Re6#
2) 1. Nf7 Rxd7 2. Re5#
3) 1. Ra8 Nc7 2. Rd8#+
4) 1. Kf8 Rb7 2. Rd8#
5) 1. Nd6 Nb6 (1. ... c4+ 2. Nxc4+
   Kb5 3. Nb2+) 2. Nb7#
6) 1. Ka3 Nd1 2. Nb3#
7) 1. Bf6 Rxf7 (1. ... Rh2 2. Bg6) 2.

Ra8#
8) 1. e5+ Bxe5 (1. ... Kc5 2. Ne6+) 2.
   Bf8#
9) 1. Qf7 Rg8 2. Qh5#
10) 1. g7 Be6 2. c4#
11) 1. Kb3 Nb6 2. Bb4#
12) Drawing

Draws

<small>AIM OF THE LESSON</small>
- revision
- going into things more deeply

<small>PRIOR KNOWLEDGE</small>
- draws (Step 3)

<small>ACQUISITION</small>

Instruction

It is important that everything which has been dealt with once should be discussed again at some appropriate time. Revision works wonders! In chess it is easy to revise a subject and nonetheless to do it in an interesting way. We simply have to crank up the degree of difficulty of the positions a bit. We give some examples of the known ways of achieving a draw. You decide according to each group whether these need to be dealt with.

Perpetual check

We shall start with the position in the diagram (⇨), which is not without interest. Promotion to a queen is out of the question on account of mate after 1. ... Qe4+. However, there will certainly be one or another of the students who finds the correct move quickly (however, almost always without having seen all the consequences!). The correct solution is found by elimination. All other moves lose, so White has to give check with **1. d8N+**. Because of all sorts of knight forks the black king has no choice. After **1. ... Kf8 2. Nde6+ Kf7 3. Nd8+** the game ends in a draw. We find a new challenge in the diagram (⇩). After allowing thinking time, ask what sort

of way to a draw works for White. "Too little material" will certainly be mentioned. That is correct, but perpetual check also plays a part. The solution: **1. Be4+! Nxe4 2. Nf4+ Kd4 3. Ne2+ Kd3 4. Nc1+ Kc3 5. Ne2+ Kb3 6. Nc1+.** The black king must keep on protecting its rook. In the diagram (⇧) too, the students will first have to weigh up various options against each other before they find the correct way. White gives perpetual check with **1. Ng6+** (and not 1. Nf7+? Kg8 2. Nxd8+ Qxe6+ 3. Nxe6 d3 4. Kf3 h3, after which Black wins) **1. ... Kh7 2. Nf8+** (possible, since the Rd8 must protect the queen) **2. ... Kh8 3. Ng6+** with a draw.

In both these examples perpetual check was made possible because a defender had to protect another piece. Other combinations can also be of help when forcing perpetual check.

In this diagram (⇨) the perpetual check appears to be somewhere in the far distance. White has no time for a mating attack 1. N5b6 Qe2+ 2. Kc1 Qe1+ 3. Kc2 Nd4# does not end well for him. Here the magnet can help: **1. Ra8+ Kxa8 2. N5b6+ Ka7 3. Nc8+.** The solution is not obvious because we do not expect that two knights can so easily give perpetual check.

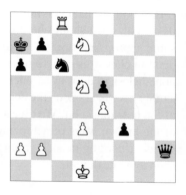

Perpetual attack

Closely related to perpetual check is the perpetual attack. That may be an attack on an important piece, but a mating threat which keeps on recurring is also a perpetual attack.

In this diagram (⇩) White has to draw. The bad position of the black king makes this possible. The students will first of all try 1. Nd6+ Kd8 2. Rf8+ Kc7. The black king gets more and more freedom of movement, so this is the wrong way. A double attack is urgently needed to help out: **1. Rh5.** After the capture on h5 it is an immediate draw. Black must play **1. ... Qb2** to save the queen and to defend against

the mate on h8. White repeats the trick with **2. Rb5 Qh2 3. Rh5**.

In this diagram (⇧) White is once more a whole rook down. Now all he has to do is win the knight on d5. With correct play a king and rook cannot defeat a king and knight. How does White win the knight? The attempt 1. Nb7 (planning 1. ... Rd7 2. Nc5) fails to 1. ... Rb6. The knight must remain close to the white king. The only way for that to work is **1. Ke5 Rd8 2. Ne6 Rd7 3. Nc5 Rd8 4. Ne6**.

In this example we can see how vulnerable a rook is whenever:
- the rook has to protect something
- the rook does not have much freedom of movement

In this diagram (⇨) the rook on d7 has more options, but nonetheless not enough. After **1. Nc5 Rd8** (or 1. ... Rd4 2. Nb3 Ra4 3. Nc5) **2. Nb7 Ra8 3. Nc5 Rd8 4. Nb7** the knight starts a perpetual attack on the rook. Otherwise Black must give up one of his two bishops.

Insufficient material
In the endgame taking all one's opponent's pawns is a good method of securing a draw. It is known that having a minor piece more is not sufficient. There are two instructive examples in this diagram (⇩). On the left, White must try to swap off the c-pawn. After 1. a7 Bb7 2. b6 c5+ 3. Kb5 Kd6 the chance has gone. White must play the immediate **1. b6**. Then clearly there follows **1. ... cxb6 2. Kb5**. But also **1. ... c5+ 2. Ka5!** (not 2. Kb5 Bd7+ 3. Ka5 Kc6 4. b7 Kc7, and White loses both pawns without his king being able to get at the c-pawn) **2. ... Kc6 3. b7 Bxb7 4. axb7 Kxb7 5. Kb5** is insufficient for Black. On the right the bishop is protecting its own pawn, so the h-pawn must lure it away. Here too the order of moves again plays an important

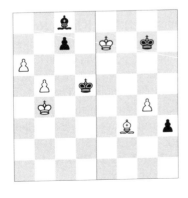

part. White wins after 1. ... h2 2. Be4, and the black king can no longer reach the white pawn (2. ... Kh6 3. Kf6). So Black must begin with **1. ... Kg6 2. Ke6 Kg5** (2. ... h2 is also possible now) **3. Ke5 h2 4. Ke3 h1Q 5. Bxh1 Kxg4.**

Stalemate

Can White draw in the position in the diagram (⇧), that is the question we ask. It is quite probable that the reply we shall get will be "That won't work". We then point out that there is actually a possibility for a draw. Which method has not yet been discussed? Stalemate! The solution will then be found quickly: **1. e4+ Kg4** (1. ... Kxe4 2. Nc5+) **2. Ne5+ fxe5** stalemate. In their own games too, it is useful for the students to consider the ways they can draw.

Avoiding stalemate

Not allowing a draw is an important technique for the side which has the most material. In the diagram (⇨) the side with the overwhelming superiority will without thinking play 1. b7. After 1. ... Rb2+ 2. Kd3 Rb3+ 3. Kc4 Rb4+ 4. Kc5 Rb5+ 5. Kc6 Rb6+ Black continues to offer to sacrifice his rook in order to force stalemate (6. Kc7 Rxb7+). We call this sort of rook a 'rampant rook'. When there is not much material on the board there is the danger of stalemating the opposing king. The correct move is **1. Rg6** (1. Rb7 also wins but White must avoid h7 for the moment!) **1. ... Kh7 2. Rc6 Rb3 3. Kd2,** and the king can support its b-pawn.

The final positions in this lesson are not difficult whenever the solution is known. Then everyone says: "Of course!" The art is to spot the problem early on. In this diagram (⇩) 1. d8Q (R) is wrong since Black is stalemated after 1. ... g2 2. Qd1 g1Q 3. Qxg1. So the correct move is **1. d8B g2 2. Bb6 Ka1 3. Bg1 Ka2 4. Bd4** with an easy win.

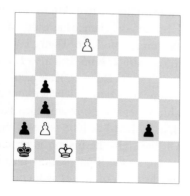

In the position in the diagram (⇧) it is also about avoiding stalemate. The presence of the black b-pawn and the freedom of movement of the black king mean that at first we certainly do not think about stalemate. White can win with **1. b5+** (1. c8Q? Rc7+ 2. Qxc7 b5+ leads to stalemate) **1. ... Kb6 2. c8N+** (2. c8Q? Rc7+ 3. Qxc7+ Kxc7 4. Kc5 b6+ 5. Kd5 Kd7 with a draw) **2. ... Kc7 3. Nxe7** winning.

Reminder
◊ *Draws*

Workbook

☐ *Draw / Stalemate: A*
Explanation: The side whose move it is can draw by stalemate. In some positions stalemate only occurs in the main variation. The stronger side can avoid the stalemate, but must also in these case head for draws either because there is insufficient material or because a level position arises. There is a mixture of easy and difficult tasks.
Mistake: The answer is wrong.
Help: What does the opponent play now?
Mistake: Task 10 is too difficult or the answer is 1. Ke1.
Help: We try out the obvious looking moves. Apparently all the moves lead to a loss because the knight h4 has no moves. Look for 1. Bxg5 and 1. Ke1 among the answers. Which move is left? A bishop move.

☐ *Draw / Insufficient material: A*
Explanation: The side whose move it is can draw by reducing the material on the board so much that the opponent no longer has have enough material to win. The clearest form of this is when the opponent has too little material to deliver mate. The positions which are not so clear for the students are those in which the opposing side finishes with an advantage in material, for example rook against knight. These positions are drawn. This has to be discussed in this lesson.

Mistake:	The task is too difficult.
Help:	Have the student explain what he saw and why he cannot get the task to work. It may be a case of not knowing enough about the distributions of material which lead to a draw.

☐ *Endgame / Avoiding stalemate: A*

Explanation: On this sheet the most obvious looking move is not the correct one, since it leads to a draw. On one occasion an intermediate move is the solution, on another a creative waiting move is required. An entertaining exercise sheet.

Mistake:	The strongest continuation is overlooked.
Help:	In position 5 1. Nf2+ followed by 2. Rxa2 is the solution. The student overlooks 1. ... Ke1.

☐ *Draw / Perpetual check: A*

Explanation: The side which has the move must bring about draws by perpetual check. If the student writes down a single repetition that is enough.

Mistake:	The solution does not lead to perpetual check.
Help:	Have the student try again.

☐ *Draw / Mix: A*

Explanation: Which form of a draw is the most probable? Working that out is more important than directly trying out different moves. Once the way to get the draw has been recognised, then the moves which come into question can be sought in a more targeted way. The subjects are perpetual check, perpetual attack, stalemate and too little material.

Mistake:	The answer is wrong.
Help:	If, after several attempts, the student still cannot find the solution, then he can be told it.

ANSWERS

☐ *Draw / Stalemate: A*

1) 1. Re1 Qxe1 stalemate (1. ... Nb3 2. Rxb1+ Kxb1 3. Kxa4)

2) 1. Rc7 Bxc7 stalemate (1. ... Nb7 2. Rxb7 Rxb7 stalemate)

3) 1. ... Qe1+ (1. ... Qf2+ 2. Qxf2 ; 1. ... Qf3+ 2. Bxf3 ; 1. ... Qf4+ 2. Bf3) 2. Kxe1 stalemate

4) 1. Qe1 Qxe1 stalemate (1. ... Bg2 2. Qxf1+ Kxf1 3. Kxg4)

5) 1. b4+ Kxb4 2. Nc6+ Nxc6 stalemate

6) 1. Qxg7+ Kxg7 2. Nxf5+ gxf5 stalemate (2. ... Kf6? 3. Nxg3)

7) 1. Rd8 Rxd8 (1. ... Kxb7? 2. Rxg8) 2. b8Q Rxb8 stalemate (2. ... Kd7?

148

3. Qxe5)

8) 1. Bh5+ Kxh5 2. g4+ Kg6 stalemate

9) 1. d8Q Bxd8 2. Bf4+ Kxf4 stalemate

10) 1. Be3 (1. Bxg5+? Kxg5) 1. ... Qxe3 2. Nf5+ Bxf5 stalemate

11) 1. Nb6 Rb8! 2. Ka1 Rxb6 stalemate (2. ... Rc8 3. Nxc8 stalemate)

12) 1. Kh4 (1. Bxc6+ Kxc6 2. Kf4 Kd6) 1. ... g5+ (1. ... Qxg2 stalemate) 2. Kh5 Qxg2 stalemate

□ *Draw / Insufficient material: A*

1) 1. ... Kf4 (1. ... Kg2? 2. h4) 2. Kd4 Kg5 3. Ne3 Kh4

2) Drawing

3) 1. Bg2 Rxh5 2. Kg4+ Rd5

4) 1. Nf6 Nh6 2. Nd7

5) 1. f4+ Kxf4 (1. ... Rxf4 2. Ne6+) 2. Nxa4

6) 1. Rb2+ Kg1 2. Ra2! Nxa2+ (2. ...
Rxa2 stalemate) 3. Kb2

7) 1. Nxf4 Bxf4 2. e4

8) 1. Bd7+ Kb4 2. g4

9) 1. Rh6 Nxh6 2. g6 Nhf5

10) 1. Ba3 bxa3 stalemate

11) 1. Ne5 Bc8 2. Nf3+

12) 1. Rxc2 Bxc2+ 2. Ka3 Nc3 3. Kb2

□ *Endgame / Avoiding stalemate: A*

1) 1. Ra5+ (1. Rxd5 stalemate?) 1. ... Qxa5 2. b7+ Ka7 3. b8Q+ Ka6 4. Qb7#

2) 1. Bg7+ (1. Rxg1? b1Q+ 2. Rxb1 stalemate) 1. ... Qxg7 2. Rh1+

3) 1. Qe1 Rxe1+ 2. Kh2

4) 1. Bg4+ (1. Bxf5? stalemate) 1. ... Qxg4 (1. ... Kxg4 2. Nh6+ Kxg3 3. Nxf5+ Kg4 4. Ke4) 2. Nf6+ Kg6 3. Nxg4

5) 1. Rf2 (1. Rxa2 stalemate ; 1. Nf2+ Ke1 2. Rxa2 stalemate) 1. ... a1Q 2. Rf1+

6) 1. Bg1 g2 2. Nf2

7) 1. Qd6 Qxd6+ 2. e5+

8) 1. g4 Qxd1+ 2. Kxd1 Kxf3 3. g5; 1. ... Qg6 2. Rd3+

9) 1. c3+ Qxc3 2. Rd8+ Kc5 3. Rc8+ Kd4 4. Rxc3 Kxc3 5. Kg5

10) 1. f7+ (1. Bxe6? stalemate) 1. ... Kxf7 (1. ... Kxe7 2. Bxe6) 2. Bh4

11) 1. Nb4 (1. Bxb6? stalemate) 1. ... Qxb4 (1. ... Qa5 2. Bd2+ Kd4 3. Nc6+ ; 1. ... Kxb4 2. Bxb6) 2. Bd2+ Kd4 3. Bxb4

12) 1. Rb4+ (1. Rxb2 Ra5+ 2. Kb7 Rb5+) 1. ... Kg5 2. Rxb2

□ *Draw / Perpetual check: A*

1) 1. ... Nf4+ (1. ... Nxg3+ 2. Ke1) 2. Kg1 Ne2+ 3. Kf1 Nf4+

2) 1. Qh8+ Kd7 (1. ... Qf8 2. Qxf6) 2. Qh3+ Ke8 3. Qh8+

3) 1. Nf5+ (1. Rxh2+ Kg5 2. Rxh8 a2 3. Rh1 a1Q 4. Rxa1 Rxa1) 1. ... Kh5 2. Ng7+ Kh6 3. Nf5+

4) 1. ... Nf5+ 2. Kf1 (2. Kh1 Ng3#) 2. ... Ne3+ 3. Kg1 (3. Ke1 Bc3#)

5) 1. ... Rd1+ (1. ... Qe1+ 2. Bf1) 2. Bxd1 Qe1+ 3. Kh2 Qh4+ 4. Kg1 Qe1+

6) 1. Bb2+ Kh6 (1. ... Kg8 2. Nf6+; 1. ... Kh7 2. Nf6+; 1. ... Kg6 2. Ne5+; 1. ... Kf7 2. Ne5+) 2. Bc1+ Kg7 (2. ... Kh5 3. Nf6+=) 3. Bb2+=

7) 1. Nd7+ Kf7 2. Ne5+ Kf6 3. Nd7+
8) 1. ... Rh1+ 2. Kf2 Rh2+
9) 1. Kf8 b1Q 2. Nf7+ Kh7 3. Nxg5+
Kh8 4. Nf7+
10) 1. Qh4+ Kg7 2. Re7+ Rxe7 3. Qxe7+
Kg8 4. Qe8+ Kg7 5. Qe7+ Kh6 6.
Qh4+
11) 1. Bd7+ Kd8 2. Bb6+ Ke7 3. Bc5+
12) 1. Rd8+ Bf8 (1. ... Kh7 2. Nf6+ Kg7
3. Nh5+) 2. Nf6+ Kg7 3. Nh5+ Kh7
4. Nf6+

□ *Draw / Mix: A*

1) Drawing
2) Drawing
3) 1. Bb3+ Kf5 2. Bc2+ Ke6 3. Bb3+
4) 1. ... Rg8 2. Ne6 Rxg7+
5) 1. Qd5+ Kxd5 stalemate (1. ... Qxd5
stalemate)
6) 1. ... Nc1+ (1. ... Nxb2 2. Bc2 Nd6
3. Rb1 Nbxc4 4. bxc4 Nxc4) 2. Ke1
Nd3+ 3. Ke2 Nc1+ 4. Ke1 Nd3+
7) 1. Kf1 Bh4 2. Ng3+ Bxg3 stalemate
8) 1. Ng5+ Kf8 (1. ... Kf6? 2. Ne4+
Ke7 3. Nxd6+) 2. Nxh7+ Kf7 (2.
... Kg8? 3. Rxe8+ Kxh7 4. Rd8) 3.
Ng5+
9) 1. Nf7+ Rxf7 2. Rg8+ Kxg8 stalemate
10) 1. Nd2 b2 2. Nc4 b1Q 3. Na3+
11) 1. Rc4 Rc2 (1. ... Qa8? 2. Rc1#) 2.
Rb4+ (2. Rxc2 Qd4+ 3. Rd2 Qg1+) 2.
... Rb2 (2. ... Qb2 3. Rxb2+ Kxb2=)
3. Rc4
12) 1. g3+ Kg4 2. Bc3 Bxc3 stalemate
(2. ... Ne7+ 3. Kh6 Bxc3 stalemate;
3. ... Nf7+ 4. Kh7 Bxc3 stalemate)

6⁺   Trapping

AIM OF THE LESSON
- learning about the move which prepares the trapping

PRIOR KNOWLEDGE
- trapping (Step 3)

ACQUISITION

Instruction
In the fourth Step no fewer than five lessons
are devoted to the five different preparatory
moves. There is a good reason for paying this so
much attention, because the preparatory move
is a strong weapon, which allows combinations
which are not yet possible to be carried out successfully. Since all forms of the double attack
have now been dealt with, employing this as a
preparatory move to 'trapping' a piece is only
a short step. We shall deal with all the forms.

Eliminating a defender
In this diagram (⇨) the queen on h3 has no
squares to which it can move. The attack with
1. Bg2 Qh5 makes no sense. The solution is
obvious: **1. e5**. Black has a choice: lose the
knight or the queen because a move by the
knight is followed with **2. Bg4**.
Also in this diagram (⇩) the queen is pretty well
shut in. It can still go to a2, 1. Rc5 achieves
nothing. The move 1. Bc4 attacks and deprives
the queen of a2, but after the bishop move the
a5-square is accessible again. So the knight
on c6 is the defending piece which is holding
the black position together. Eliminating it by
capturing **1. Rxc6** is the solution. After **1. ...
bxc6 2. Bc4** the queen is trapped.

We can make use of all forms of eliminating the defender: capturing, luring, chasing away, interfering and blocking. All these forms appear in the exercises.

We can even trap pieces on a nearly empty board. In the diagram (⇧) the black bishop is on the edge of the board, but can still go to a lot of squares on the f1-a6 diagonal. White deprives the bishop of this option by **1. Nc6+ Kb5 2. Nb8**. The king on b5 is getting in the way of its own bishop!

Chasing
At the level of Step 2 we sometimes met pieces which got shut in like after **1. e4 c5 2. Bb5? a6 3. Ba4? b5 4. Bb3 c4**. A perfect example of chasing. A piece does not have much freedom of movement and gets into more and more problems. Pieces can also be cut off in the middle of the board like this. In the diagram (⇨) the bishop on d3 is lost after **1. ... c4 2. Be4 f5**. It is bad luck for White that after 2. Bxb6 Black recaptures on b6 with check.

There is a much harder example in the following diagram (⇩). First of all we must work out which piece is going to be the victim. It is the black queen. It still has three free squares at its disposal (apart from the square on which it is standing). With **1. Na4** White not only attacks the queen, but at the same time deprives it of the squares c5 and b2. Black must play **1. ... Qb4**. Now the knight is attacked; a move like 2. a3 is not good enough. However, **2. Rd4** is good. The rook move attacks the queen and protects the knight on a4.

Targeting
Targeting consists of an attack + a threat. Of course all the pieces can 'target' another, but the

pawn is particularly well suited to do so. Indeed, a large proportion is accounted for the pawn.

In the diagram (⇧) Black's queen is somewhat unfortunately posted on e7. It is cutting off the retreat for the bishop on f6. White takes advantage of this with **1. e4 Nb6 2. e5**. A bit surprising, normally a bishop on f6 is standing rather safe.

The cause of the problem in the loss of material is often the unfortunate position of your own pieces in your own half of the board. In the diagram (⇨) White has just played Re1. Not only is that not a sensible move (the idea of Nf1 does not work on account of Nb3), but it is also even a bad one. The knight on f3 now has no squares left to move to. Since both sides are manoeuvring in their own half of the board, everything seems just fine. However Black wins a piece **1. ... g5 2. Bg3 g4** or **2. Be3 g4**. In both cases the black queen and the bishop are each covering h4 or g5.

Clearing

In clearing too, one of your own pieces is getting in the way, though now it can be seen in a positive way. The piece is preventing an opposing piece from being trapped. When there is a double attack in the offing, the clearing move must be played with tempo. This is usually not necessary when trapping. In the diagram (⇩) the black queen's retreat is cut off. All the escape squares are in White's hands. However, White does not have all the time in the world because Black is threatening to free his queen with Ba6 (the c4-square becomes available). The solution is not difficult. The white queen is preventing the possibility of Nd2. The b2-pawn must still be protected, so **1. Qc1** I obvious. The threat of **2. Nd2** is decisive.

The situation in this diagram (⇧) often occurs. White tries to attack with too few pieces, but does not realise this. He plays (the bad) **1. h5**, to open the h-file. Black can of course simply parry the attack with moves like 1. ... Qe8 or 1. ... Rf7. There are enough defenders. However, Black has something even better and keeps the position closed with **1. ... g5**. The white queen's retreat is shut off. Black is now threatening to free the g8-square for the knight with **2. ... Kh8**. Even **2. f4** does not help against this, since **2. ... Kh8 3. fxg5 Ng8** still costs the queen.

Luring (attracting)

A capture (exchange or sacrifice) lets us entice a piece on to a fatal square on the board. In the diagram (⇨) there is an easy example. White lures the black queen into the trap with **1. Rxd3 Qxd3 2. Bf1**. Of course Black must not recapture on d3, then he has a piece less in any case.

The position in the diagram (⇩) is slightly more difficult. It is Black's move. It does not appear that any piece can be shut in. Now we know that there is a way to win. The move **1. ... g4** is of course obvious, but after the capture on g4 the trapping of the queen looks to be far away. But with **2. ... e5** Black can capture the queen with a discovered attack (see also Step 3+). The attack is delivered by the bishop on d7, and the pawn on e5 deprives the queen of the f4-square.

Luring is treated as the last preparatory move in this chapter. That is because it is the most difficult one.

Reminder

◊   *Trapping*

Workbook

☐   *Mobility / Trapping (chasing): A*
  Explanation: The target is a piece which does not have much freedom of
         movement. Which piece does not have many escape squares?
         The victim can be chased on to a fatal square and trapped.
  Mistake: The task is too difficult.
  Help: Set up the position. Which piece is the victim? Only point it out
         if the student cannot manage the task.

☐   *Mobility / Trapping (eliminating the defence): B*
  Explanation: The target is a piece which does not have much freedom of move-
         ment. Which piece does not have many escape squares? Trapping
         one immediately is impossible. Another piece is preventing this.
         Eliminate the defender, trap the piece and hey presto!
  Mistake: The "trapped" piece can still move.
  Help: Have the student find the defensive option. How do you eliminate
         this possibility?

☐   *Mobility / Trapping (targeting): C*
  Explanation: The target is a piece which does not have much freedom of move-
         ment. Which piece does not have many escape squares? A piece
         can have its options shut down with tempo and then be trapped.
  Mistake: The student cannot find the answer.
  Help: Ask targeted questions. Show the student a piece that does not
         have much freedom of movement. Which square must you still
         take away from it? Can that be done with tempo?

☐   *Mobility / Trapping (luring): D*
  Explanation: Once more we have to trap a piece. The difficulty is that – com-
         pared to the other practice sheets on trapping – this time the piece
         may have enough freedom of movement. That makes this sheet
         of exercises a bit more difficult. Yet the task is easy: lure the
         piece on to a fatal square and shut it in. This can be done with a
         clever sacrifice (it is only in position 8 that there is an exchange).
  Mistake: The task is too difficult.

Help: What have you already tried? Which piece do you think you can trap?

☐ *Mobility / Trapping (clearing): E*
Explanation: The target is a piece which does not have much freedom of movement. Which piece does not have many escape squares? One of your own pieces is getting in the way. You have to move it away with tempo so that the trapping of a piece is made possible.
Mistake: In position 4 the solution given is 1. Rf1.
Help: Praise the move because it threatens 2. Nd1. Have the student look for the refutation of the rook move (1. ... Rd7 or even 1. ... g4). Is the rook required after 2. Nd1? No, so make a better move with the rook.

☐ *Mobility / Trapping (mix): F*
Explanation: The target is a piece which does not have much freedom of movement. Which piece does not have many escape squares? A piece can be trapped after a preparatory move (see exercise pages A-E).

ANSWERS

☐ *Mobility / Trapping (chasing): A*
1) 1. Bd2 Qc5 (1. ... Qa4 2. b3) 2. Bb4 (2. b4? Qxf2)
2) 1. Rb3 Qa4 2. Bb5
3) 1. ... Bf4 2. Qd3 Bf5
4) 1. Ng3 Qg4 2. h3
5) 1. Rb3 Qa5 2. Bb6
6) 1. Rb5 Qxc3 2. Bb2
7) 1. ... Bg5 2. Qd3 Ne5

8) 1. ... d4 2. Qf4 g5
9) 1. Bf4 Qd5 2. c4
10) 1. g4 Qa5 (1. ... Qf6 2. Bg5) 2. Bd2
11) 1. e4 Be6 (1. ... Bxe4 2. Nxe4) 2. d5
12) 1. Nd2 Qb2 2. Ra2

☐ *Mobility / Trapping (eliminating the defence): B*
1) 1. Bxf7+ Nxf7 2. Ne6
2) 1. Rxf5 gxf5 2. Kd2 Rxc4 3. bxc4
3) 1. Rxc8 Rxc8 2. b3
4) 1. Nxf6+ Qxf6 2. f5
5) 1. ... Bd4+ 2. Kh1 h4
6) 1. ... Rh5 2. Bxh5 g5

7) 1. Bxf6 Bxf6 2. f4
8) 1. a5 Nxc4 2. Bxc4 Qxc4 3. Ra4
9) 1. ... b5 2. Nc5 Ra3
10) 1. Bxd4 exd4 2. Na4
11) 1. Nc4 Qf5 2. f3
12) 1. Re1 Kf7 2. f5

□ *Mobility / Trapping (targeting): C*
1) 1. f4 Nd7 2. f5
2) 1. ... Bh6+ 2. Kb1 Bf4
3) 1. g4
4) Drawing
5) 1. ... Rf4+ 2. Kg1 Rf8
6) 1. ... Nf4 2. Bf1 Bf8

7) 1. Nf5 Bd8 2. Nh4
8) 1. Be7 Rd7 2. Bg5
9) 1. ... Ne5 2. Bb3 Bg4
10) 1. Rd8+ Kh7 2. Bd6
11) 1. Bd6 Rd8 2. b3
12) 1. e5 Ne4 2. Na4

□ *Mobility / Trapping (luring): D*
1) 1. ... axb4 2. Qxa8 Nb6
2) 1. f6 Qxf6 2. Bg5
3) 1. e5 Qxe5 2. Bf4
4) 1. ... g5 2. Qxh5 Bg4
5) 1. ... c6 2. Qxc6+ Bd7
6) 1. ... axb5 2. Qxa8 Nb6

7) 1. Rxe4 Qxe4 2. Bc6
8) 1. ... Nxe5 2. Qxe5 Rd5
9) 1. b6 Bxb6 2. Nd5
10) 1. ... axb4 2. Bxb4 c5
11) 1. c3 Qxc3+ 2. Bd2
12) 1. b4 Qxb4 2. Nc6

□ *Mobility / Trapping (clearing): E*
1) 1. ... Nxf3+ 2. Bxf3 Bf6
2) 1. Nxd5 exd5 2. Bc7
3) 1. e5 Bxe5 2. Bf3
4) 1. Rxd8 (1. Rf1 Rd7) 1. ... Nxd8
   2. Nd1
5) 1. Ng5+ Rxg5 2. Bd1
6) 1. Kh1 fxg4 2. Ng1

7) 1. g4 fxg4 2. Ng3
8) 1. e5 dxe5 2. Ne4
9) 1. Qd1 Ne4 2. Be1
10) 1. ... Qd8 (1. ... Qc8 2. Nc4 Be8)
    2. Nc4 Be8
11) 1. ... Bh4 2. Qf1 f6
12) 1. d6 Bxd6 2. Nd5

□ *Mobility / Trapping (mix) F*
1) 1. ... c5 2. Qd1 c4
2) 1. a3
3) 1. Nxe4 Qxe4 2. Bf3
4) 1. ... f5 2. Bd3 f4
5) 1. ... Rf7
6) 1. Bg5 hxg5 2. hxg5

7) 1. ... Nxe4 2. fxe4 Be5
8) 1. d5 cxd5 2. f5
9) 1. ... Ng4 2. Re2 f6
10) 1. Bxf6 Bxf6 2. f4
11) 1. Rxe5 Qxe5 2. Bf4
12) 1. Bg5 Qf5 2. g4

Mini-plans

AIM OF THE LESSON
- learning to select a move in a targeted fashion

PRIOR KNOWLEDGE
- lessons on mini-plans

ACQUISITION

Instruction

Earlier, we were taught that a bad plan is better than no plan at all. What a wonderful excuse to justify bad moves when the game is finished! At this level it is still better to think in terms of moves. Consider your move with great care. In this diagram (⇨) it is Black's move. For the moment the white pieces are more active. Only the white king is still vulnerable in the middle. This factor is so striking that 1. ... Qe7+ is a popular suggestion. White's reply is totally unexpected: 2. Kf1 (2. Be3 Ne4 and 2. Qe3 Qxe3+ 3. Bxe3 Nxd5 are good for Black). Neither 2. ... b5 3. Re1 nor does 2. ... Qe4 3. Bxf6 Qxd4 Bxd4 4. c4 bring Black any further forward. Black must first play **1. ... b5** (deactivate your opponent's active pieces). It is of course pure luck that after **2. Bb3 Re8+** is possible. After **3. Kf1** Black also, by means of **3. ... h6**, forces the active bishop on g5, to make up its mind. The bishop must go back to c1, so as to protect b2, since 4. Bh4 g5 5. Bg3 Ne4 is even worse. Let us compare the position after **4. Bc1 Ne4** with the starting position, and we see that the activity of the white pieces has become much less, whereas that of the black pieces has clearly increased. But where do things go now? Work out a new mini-plan; e.g. put the queen on f6

and double the rooks on the e-file (according to what White does).

In the diagram (⇧) Black is threatening Bxf3. That not only menaces the pawn structure, but also the protection of d4. The passive 1. Be2 Rhe8 2. Ng5 Qd7 3. Bxg4 Nxg4 does not achieve much. The active **1. Ne5** is much better. The attack on f7 means that d4 is indirectly protected. Black has to protect f7: with **1. ... Qe6** (going into the battery) or with **1. ... Be6**. The queen move is followed by **2. h3** (2. Ng6 Ne4) **2. ... Bh5 3. Qf4!** and the threats **4. Bf5** and **4. Ng6** can no longer be parried. **1... Be6** is followed by **2. Nb5 Qe7 3. Nxc6 bxc6**, and now **4. Nxa7+ Kd7! 5. Qa5 Ra8** is not quite clear. Can the knight escape or not? If there is one, choose the safer way: **4. Nc3** (planning Na4) gives White a clear advantage (better pawn structure).

It is also important to choose the safe way in clearly superior positions. In this diagram (⇨) the fight does not continue much longer after **1. Rad1** (bring up your pieces!). White continues with **2. Qxh6** or **2. Re3**. The player with White decided on the illogical 1. Nf5 Bxf5 (lets an attacking piece be swapped off for an undeveloped piece) 2. Qxf5 Qxc2 3. Re3, and now after 3. ... Rad8 (instead of 3. ... Rf8 which loses at once) the struggle would have been completely open; i.e. 4. Rg3+ Kf8 5. Qh7 Rd1+ 6. Rxd1 Qxd1+ 7. Kh2 Qd6.

In this diagram (⇩) Black is slightly worse on account of the doubled pawns on the c-file. They cannot be resolved easily. In addition, the fixed pawn on e5 (on a black square) is a slight disadvantage. But all that is not catastrophic. Black needs to be patient with **1. ... Be7**. If White wants to make progress, then pawns have to be exchanged and there is again more space for the bishop. When you have a dark-squared bishop it is to your advantage to place your pawns on white squares. The workload is divided in the following way: The bishop controls the black squares, the pawns the white ones. The player with Black moved **1. ... dxe4**. Not a good move. Black is left with only isolated pawns on the queenside. In addition the c4-square is conceded to the knight. After **2. dxe4 Be7 3. Nc4 f6 4. Rad1 Kb7 5. Rxd8 Rxd8 6. Rd1** White should be trying to exchange the last rook. White has good chances. Have the students play out the position to a finish (simultaneous or against one another).

Analyse above all games by the students which involve positions of the type with a 'mini-plan'. In a game there are enough suitable moments.

1. e4 e5 2. f4 Nc6 3. Nf3

In lesson 2[+] we already learned about 3. fxe5 Qh4+.

3. ... Nf6

What is the best move? White can win some tempi with 4. fxe5 Nxe4 5. d3 (most surprisingly, few students find this move) 5. ... Nc5 6. d4 Ne4 7. d5 (better than 7. Qe2 f5 8. exf6 d5) 7. ... Ne7 8. Bc4 d6 9. Qe2 with the advantage.

4. Nc3 exf4 5. d4 d5 6. e5 Ne4 7. Bxf4 Bb4 8. Bd2 (see diagram ⇨)

8. ... Nxd2

So far Black has played excellently. The move played is not bad, but why should you release the tension? One good move is 8. ... Bg4, because Black need not fear 9. Nxe4 dxe4.

9. Qxd2 0-0 10. Bd3 Bg4 11. h3?

Many players avoid tension. The correct move is 11. 0-0.

11. ... Bxf3 12. gxf3 Qh4+ 13. Qf2 (see diagram ⇩).

Which moves should be considered? Three

160

captures. The students quickly realise that 13. ... Nxd4 is the best (and most amusing) move. In fact after 14. Qxh4 Nxf3+ 15. Kf2 Nxh4 16. Nxd5 Bc5+ 17. Kg3 Ng6 Black is well placed. Probably 13. ... Qxd4 14. Qxd4 Nxd4 15. f4 c6, also with a major advantage, is objectively even better. We have kept the worst of the three moves for the game.

13. ... Qxf2+ 14. Kxf2 Nxd4 15. Nxd5 Bc5 16. b4 Bb6 17. Nxb6 cxb6 18. f4 Rac8 19. c4 f6
(see diagram ⇑)
A good move. Black has to make space for his rooks. In addition, the fact that the white pawn structure is weakened is important.

20. Ke3 fxe5 21. fxe5 Rcd8
The double attack 21. ... Nc6 nets a pawn. Also, when we look at the future course of the game, the player with Black appears to be thinking that no combinations are possible in the endgame.

22. Rhf1
Better is 22. Be4.

22. ... Nc6 23. Rxf8+ Rxf8 24. Rf1 Nxb4?
It would have been cleverer to exchange on f8 first.

25. Bxh7+
Every trainer faces this atrocious circumstance. His student has played well all through the game and then throws it away with a moment of carelessness.

PRACTICE

Reminder
◊   *Mini-plans*

Workbook

☐   *Mini-plans / Increasing activity: A*
    Explanation: Not much is won on this sheet. The correct move clearly restricts the activity of at least one piece.
    Mistake: The student does not find the correct answer.

Help: Can you find a more active position for this piece? And for this one?

☐ *Mini-plans / Exploiting the vulnerability: A*
Explanation: The opponent is vulnerable somewhere on the board: a piece which is hard to defend or a square or a threat which is hard to parry. Take advantage of the weakness.
Mistake: The answer is wrong.
Help: Ask the students to list the opponent's weaknesses.

☐ *Mini-plans / Exploiting the vulnerability: B*
Explanation: See exercise page A.

☐ *Mini-plans / Opening the position: A*
Explanation: One of your own pawns is getting in your way. Sacrifice the pawn or force your opponent to take it.
Mistake: The position is too difficult.
Help: Which pawn would you most like to see out of the way?

ANSWERS

☐ *Mini-plans / Increasing activity: A*
1) 1. Rc1 Nbd7 (1. ... Bd8 2. Nd5
   Qxa2 3. Nc7+) 2. Nd5
2) 1. ... Nb4 2. Qb3 Nd3+
3) 1. Ng3 (followed by 2. Ne4)
4) 1. Be7 (1. Qxh4? Qd7) 1. ... Rc7
   2. Bf6 Kf8 3. Qxh4 Ke8 4. Qh7
5) 1. Nb5 Qb6 2. Nd6+

6) 1. Nb5 Qd8 2. Nd6
7) 1. Bg5 Qd7 2. Bf6+ Kg8 3. Qd2
8) 1. Ne4 Bb8 2. Nd6
9) 1. ... Nd5 2. Qf2 f5 3. Qf3 Ne3
10) 1. Qd6! (1. Qd2 d5)
11) Drawing
12) Drawing

☐ *Mini-plans / Exploiting the vulnerability: A*
1) 1. ... Bf8 and 2. ... Bc5
2) 1. Re1 Rxc1 2. Bxc1
3) 1. Bd1 and 2. Bb3
4) 1. Ba5 (threatens 2. Bxb6 and 2. c5)
5) 1. Qf4 Bg7 2. Rxe7+ Kxe7 3. Qf7+
6) 1. Nb5 Nf8 2. Nc7
7) 1. ... Ba3 2. Bxa3 Qxc3+

8) 1. ... Bb7 and 2. ... Ba6+
9) 1. ... Ba6 (threatens 2. .. Bxc3 of 2. ... Bxe2) 2. Na4 Qb5 and Black always wins material, i.e. 3. Nac3 Bxc3 4. Nxc3 Qxf1+ 5. Qxf1 Bxf1 6. Rxf1
10) 1. ... Bg5 2. h4 Bh6
11) 1. ... Rag8 2. g3 Bxf3
12) 1. Qc1 Nh5 2. g3

☐ *Mini-plans / Exploiting the vulnerability: B*
1) 1. Qg3 Bg6 2. Qe5
2) 1. Qa3 (the a7-pawn cannot be protected: 1. ... a6 2. Rxb6 or 1. ... Ra8 2. Rxb6)
3) 1. ... Bxd4 2. Qxd4 Qc6
4) 1. ... Qa8 2. Ke2 (2. Bd1 Bc6) 2. ... Bg4
5) 1. Na4 Qc7 (1. ... Rae8 2. Nxb6) 2. Ne6
6) 1. Ng3 Qd7 2. Nxf5
7) 1. ... Bh5
8) 1. Bxh6 Bxh6 2. Qb3
9) 1. ... a4 2. Bc2 Qd5; 1. ... c4? 2. Qxd4
10) 1. Nh4 f5 2. Rxg6+
11)
12) 1. Qd6 Bg7 2. Nxc7+ Kf8 3. Nxa8

☐ *Mini-plans / Opening the position: A*
1)   1. ... e4 2. dxe4 (2. Nd2 exd3 3. exd3 Re8+ 4. Kd1 Qe7) 2. ... fxe4 3. Nd2 Qxf2+
2) 1. e5 Ng8 2. exd6
3) 1. e6 fxe6 2. Qh5+ g6 3. Qh3
4) 1. ... f6 White cannot prevent a loss of material.
5) 1. ... h5 2. h3 hxg4 3. hxg4 Rh4 4. f3 Rah8
6) 1. ... Bxd5 2. exd5 (2. Qxd5 Qh4+ ; 2. Nxd5 Qxb2 3. 0-0 Rab8) 2. ... Rfe8+
7) 1. ... f6 2. exf6 Qxf6
8) 1. d5 Nxd5 2. Nxd5 cxd5 3. Rxd5 Qe8 4. Rd7
9) 1. ... f6 2. exf6 Rxf6
10) 1. f4 gxf4 2. Bxf4
11) 1. ... f5
12) 1. d4 exd3 2. Qxd3+

163

8⁺   **Pawn endings**

AIM OF THE LESSON
* deepening existing knowledge

PRIOR KNOWLEDGE
* pawn endings (Step 3⁺, lesson 15)
* defending

ACQUISITION

Instruction
In this lesson we do a short revision of some techniques already dealt with in lesson 15. We take a particularly thorough look at defending in pawn endings.

We ask the group to name the weapons (techniques) which we can employ in pawn endings (activate the king, keep the opposing king at a distance, create passed pawns, advance the candidate, distant or protected passed pawns, etc.).

In this diagram (⇨) it is Black's move. The white b-pawn can no longer be saved. You must choose the correct way: **1. ... Ke4** (keeping at a distance) **2. Kg3 Kd3 3. Kf3 Kc2 4. Ke2 Kxb2**, and Black occupies a key square and wins. 1. ... Kd4 would be bad: 2. Kf4 Kd3 3. Ke5 Kc2 4. Kd5, and White gets there in time.

Prevent counter-play
In the diagram (⇩) Black once more has the advantage. The pawn on c3 falls, and the rest appears to be child's play. Black does win, but only if he pays attention. After the logical but badly thought-out 1. ... Kc4 2. f5! gxf5 (2. ... g5? 3. hxg5 fxg5 4. f6) 3. Kf4 Black still merely draws, since White only has the h-pawn

left. Black must first remove any counter-play from the position.
The correct move is **1. ... f5 2. Kf3 Kc4 3. Ke2 Kxc3 4. Ke3 Kc4 5. Kf3 Kd4**, and the f-pawn is soon lost.

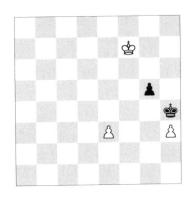

In this diagram (⇧) White must also first prevent Black's counter-play before he can set off with the e-pawn. After 1. e4? Kxh3 2. e5 g4 the pawns arrive at the same time. So the white king must attack the g-pawn. The correct way is **1. Kf6! Kxh3 2. Kxg5** or **1. ... g4 2. hxg4 Kxg4 3. e4 Kf4 4. e5**. The temptation to play 1. Kg6? remains strong, but after 1. ... g4 2. hxg4 Kxg4 3. Kf6 Kf3 the win is in the far distance.

Zugzwang
Zugzwang is an important motif in pawn endings. You soon run out of pawn moves, and so king moves (since there are no other pieces) are soon the only possible moves left. A wrong king move can rapidly cost half a point or even a whole point. It is important to devote a lot of attention to mastering the technique of 'making use of zugzwang'.

In this diagram (⇨) White can win the black f-pawn. After **1. Kg4!** Black has two possibilities, but both are hopeless: **1. ... Ke5 2. f3 Ke6 3. Kxf4 Kf6 4. Ke4 Ke6 5. Kd3** or **1. ... f3 2. Kg3 Ke5 3. Kxf3 Kf5 4. Ke3**. In both cases the white king goes to a5 and lures the black king away with the help of the f-pawn. Show on the demonstration board that the counter-attack on a4 is too slow. This is a good revision of the queen versus pawn ending.

In this diagram (⇩) Black still has available a tempo move with his b-pawn. The fact that the pawn can choose to advance either two moves or one move is a great advantage and makes the difference between a win and a draw. 1. ... b5 is bad: 2. axb5 Kxb5 3. Kb3, and Black can

make no further progress. The correct way is
**1. ... b6 2. Kb3 b5 3. axb5 Kxb5 4. Kc3 Ka4
5. Kd3 Kb4 6. Kd2 Kc4 6. Ke3 Kc3**, and the
d-pawn falls. This is a typical way of winning
a fixed pawn.

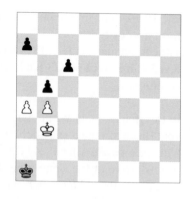

This diagram (⇑) comes from a game between
two young players. Unsuspectingly, Black
played **1. ... a6 2. axb5 axb5 3. Ka3 Kb1 4.
Kb3 Kc1 5. Kc3 Kd1 6. Kd3**, and had to be
satisfied with a draw. The possibility for White
on move two of choosing between capturing the
b-pawn and advancing beyond it is also a strong
weapon when you are working with zugzwang
(if the black king had been on b1, then advancing
would have been the correct move). There was
a win after **1. ... bxa4+ 2. Kxa4 Ka2 3. b5 c5
4. Ka5 Kb3 5. Ka6 Kb4.**
Thanks to the tempo move which Black has
with his a-pawn, he can also win with **1. ...
Kb1 2. a5 a6 3. Kc3 Ka2 4. Kd4 Kb3 5. Kc5
Kc3 6. Kxc6 Kxb4 7. Kb6 Ka4 8. Kxa6 b4 9.
Kb6 b3 10. a6 b2 11. a7 b1Q+ 12. Kc7 Qe4
13. Kb8 Kb5 14. a8Q Qe5+ 15. Kb7 Qe7+ 16.
Kc8 Qe8+ 17. Kb7 Qd7+ 18. Kb8 Kb6**. We
can gladly skip this extra way to win the game.

Defending
Enough winning techniques. Let us now concen-
trate on defence. We have an old acquaintance
when it comes to getting a draw: our opponent
has a rook pawn. In the diagram (⇨) Black
exchanges in a flash all the pawns which are
not rook pawns: **1. ... e5** (and not 1. ... e6 2.
Kh4 Kf6 3. Kg4 Kf7 4. Kg5 Kg7 5. h6+, and
White wins) **2. fxe5 Kxe5** with an easy draw
since the king reaches the corner.
And a final example with a rook pawn (there
are twelve exercises in the workbook). In this
diagram (⇩) the black king must hurry to the
corner as soon as possible, so as to shut in the

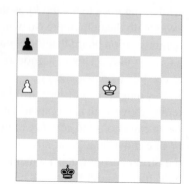

white king (actually getting into the corner itself would be asking too much). However, it must prevent the white king from holding it up along the way. There is only one correct way after c8: **1. ... Kd2 2. a6** (or 2. Kd4 Ke2) **2. ... Ke3 3. Kd5 Kf4 4. Kc6 Ke5 5. Kb7 Kd6 6. Kxa7 Kc7** with a draw.

Defending key squares is another way of achieving a draw. In this diagram (⇧) moves by White's king are not sufficient. 1. Kb2 is followed by 1. ... c5, and the king can no longer reach the pawn in time. Nor is 1. Kd2 Kf7 2. c4 b4 3. c5 Ke6 any better, since White arrives too late. A temporary pawn sacrifice offers the saving grace: **1. c4 b4** (1. ... bxc4 2. Kc2 is of course a draw with correct play – see Step 3) **2. c5** (necessary, otherwise 2. ... c5) **2. ... Kf7 3. Kb2 Ke6 4. Kb3 Kd5 5. Kxb4 c6 6. Kb3!**. The final subtlety.

In this diagram (⇨) White draws in a similar way. He starts with **1. f4**, then the rest is child's play. The mistake **1. Kg4?** has interesting consequences. Have the students try out this line against one another and then deal with the various possibilities: **1. ... Kg6 2. Kh3 Kf5!** (2. ... f5 gives away the win) **3. Kg3 Ke6!** (only move; 3. ... Ke5 4. Kg4 followed by 5. f4 is a draw) **4. Kg4** (or 4. f4 Kf5 5. fxg5 Kxg5 6. Kf3 Kf5 7. Kg3 Ke4 winning) **4. ... Ke5 5. Kg3 Kf5**, and the rest is simple.

In the following position (diagram ⇩) the defending side cannot exchange a pawn. He must work out in advance what his opponent will play. Black will get the f5-square for his king and can then advance one of his pawns. The result is an endgame with just one pawn. White must stop it in time and choose the correct route with his king in order to be able to defend the key squares. The correct way is **1. Kg3! Kf5 2. Kf3 e5 3. fxe5 Kxe5 4. Kg4** with a draw. The

wrong way would be 1. Kf3 Kf5 2. Kg3 g5 3. fxg5 Kxg5 4. Kf3 Kf5 5. Ke3 Ke5 6. Kd3 Kf4, and Black wins.

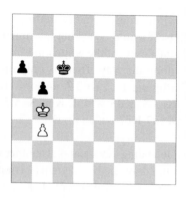

At the level of Step 4 children can play to a finish the ending of king + pawn against king correctly. The defender has to save the day by stalemate. This is a method which can also be helpful in other situations.

In the diagram (⇧) Black cannot avoid the draw after **1. Ka5** (1. Kc3 Kd5 2. Kd3 a5 loses) **1. ... Kb7 2. b4**. The best move is **2. ... Ka7** stalemate. After 2. ... Kc7 3. Kxa6 Kc6 4. Ka5 Kc7! He himself is suddenly the defender. Using stalemate to save the game is necessary, since 2. Kb4 loses after 2. ... Kb6 3. Kc3 Ka5!. Putting the king in front of the pawns first of all is frequently the correct way to play. The pawns can be moved forward later, but they can never be moved backwards!

We ask the students how many white moves in this diagram (⇨) lead to a draw. There is a great chance of getting wrong answers. 1. hxg3 hxg3 2. Ke1 Ke3 3. Kf1 Kf3 4. Kg1 g2 would lose. **1. Kf1 Kf3 2. Kg1 g2 3. h3 Kg3** leads to a draw by stalemate. The third possibility **1. h3** looks unattractive, but, surprisingly, also leads to a draw. Black cannot win on account of the edge of the board. The danger of stalemate plays a trick on Black: **1. ... Kf4 2. Kf1 Kf3 3. Kg1 g2 4. Kh2 Kf2** stalemate.

Positive aspects for the attacking side can also turn out to be helpful for the defender. A well-known example is the protected passed pawn. In this diagram (⇩) White is hopelessly lost after 1. Ka6 Kxf5 2. Kxa7 Kg4 3. Kb6 Kxg3 4. h5 Kg4 5. h6 gxh6. After the much better move **1. f6** (the pawn is lost anyway) **1. ... gxf6**, the white h-pawn has turned into a protected passed pawn. The game is drawn after **2. Ka6 f5 3. Kxa7 Kxg3 4. h5**.

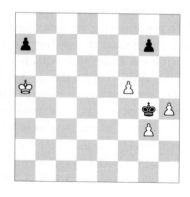

168

In this lesson we dealt with defensive techniques. These were in order: defending key squares, keeping the opposing king at a distance, stopping your own king from being kept at a distance, drawing thanks to a rook pawn and stalemate.

Reminder
◊ *Defending in pawn endings*

Workbook

☐ *Pawn endings / Technique: A*
  Explanation: This sheet of exercises contains tasks with techniques which have already been dealt with: advancing the candidate, keeping at a distance, using zugzwang, seizing key squares and avoiding stalemate. Many of the positions are suitable for playing to a finish. While working on them it is useful to play some of the positions to a finish all together.
  Mistake: The solution is wrong.
  Help: Get the students to find the mistake themselves. Possibly set up the position and all play it to a finish together.

☐ *Pawn endings / Defending: A*
  Explanation: In a pawn ending there are various techniques which the defending side can make use of. Some of them are named in the reminder.
  Mistake: The task is too difficult.
  Help: Why can a way not be found to draw? What is the problem?

☐ *Pawn endings / Defending (rook pawn): B*
  Explanation: This sheet only deals with the defensive side of things.
       - The defending king must reach the corner.
       - The defending king must reach the c8-square (find the correct route and avoid being kept at a distance).
       - By changing direction, lumber the opponent with a rook pawn.
  Mistake: The solution is wrong.
  Help: Check whether the student has mastered the correct knowledge. Looking for something about which you know nothing does not make a lot of sense.

□ *Pawn endings / Technique: A*

1) 1. ... h5 (1. ... Ke5 2. Kg4 a5 3. bxa5 bxa5 4. a4 Kf6 5. Kh5 Kxf5 6. Kxh6 g4 7. hxg4+ Kxg4 8. Kg6 Kf4) 2. f6 Ke6 3. Ke4 Kxf6 4. b5 Ke6 5. a4 Kd6 6. Kd4 g4 0-1

2) 1. Kd5 (1. Kc5 Ke6 2. Kc4 Kd6 3. Kxc3 Kc5) 1. ... Kf6 2. Kd4 Ke6 3. Kxc3 Kd5 4. Kb4 1-0

3) 1. a4 Kg8 2. b4 Kf7 3. a5 1-0

4) 1. ... cxb3 (1. ... c3+ 2. Kc2 and the black king can no longer enter) 2. Kxb3 Kc5 3. Kc2 Kc4 0-1

5) 1. Kd3 Kc5 2. g3 1-0

6) 1. e4+ dxe4+ 2. Ke3 Ke6 3. Kxe4 Kd6 4. Kf5 (of 4. f5) 1-0

7) 1. e4 (1. e3 Kd5) 1. ... dxe3 2. Kxe3 1-0

8) Drawing

9) 1. Kh2 (1. Kf2 Kh3 2. c7 Kh2 3. c8Q g1Q+ 4. Kxf3=) 1. ... Kf4 2. c7 Ke3 3. c8Q 1-0

10) 1. f4 (1. Ke3 e5 2. f4 e4) 1-0

11) 1. g5 (1. Ka8 Kc8 2. g5 hxg5 3. g4) 1. ... hxg5 (1. ... h5 2. g3 Kc8 3. Kb6 Kb8 4. Kc6) 2. g4 Kc8 3. Kb6 1-0

12) 1. g4+ (1. a4 Ke4 2. Kg2 – 2. g4 h5 – 2. ... h5 3. Kh3 g5) 1. ... Ke5 2. g5 Kd5 3. Kg2 Kc4 4. Kf3 Kb4 5. Ke4 Ka3 6. Ke5 Kxa2 7. Kf6 Kb3 8. Kg7 Kc4 9. Kxh7 1-0

□ *Pawn endings / Defending: A*

1) 1. b5 b6 (1. ... Kb4 2. b6 Kb5 3. Kc3 Kxb6 4. Kb4=) 2. Kd2 Kc4 3. Kc2 Kxb5 4. Kb3

2) 1. Kf2 (1. b4 e4 2. Kf2 Kd2 3. b5 e3+ 4. Kf3 e2 5. b6 e1Q) 1. ... Kd2 2. Kf3 Kd3 3. Kf2 e4 4. Ke1 Kc3

3) 1. g6 (1. Kh5? d3 2. g6 d2 3. g7 d1Q+) 1. ... Kxg6 2. Kg4

4) 1. Kf2 (1. Kg3 f4+ 2. Kf2 g3+ 3. Kf1 Kf5 4. Ke2 Ke5 5. Kf1 Kd4 6. Ke2 Kc3 7. Kf1 Kd2) 1. ... Kf4 2. fxg4 fxg4 3. Kg2 g3 4. Kg1 Kg4 5. Kg2 Kh4 6. Kg1 Kh3 7. Kh1 g2+ 8. Kg1 Kg3 stalemate

5) 1. ... Kg2 (1. ... e4 2. Kd6 Kg2 3. Kd5 Kf3 4. Kd4 and White wins) 2. Kd6 Kf3 3. Kxe5

6) 1. Kh8! (1. Kf8? Kf6 2. Kg8 Ke5)

7) 1. ... Kh5 2. Kxf4 Kxh4

8) 1. ... Ka4! (1. ... Kb4? 2. b3) 2. b3+ Kb4

9) 1. b5! axb5 2. b4 Kb1 stalemate

10) 1. Ka8!

11) 1. e5! (1. Kf5 Kd3) 1. ... fxe5+ 2. Kxe5

12) 1. Kb3! (1. c4? bxc3ep) 1. ... Ke2 2. c4! (2. c3? a2! 3. Kxa2 bxc3) 2. ... bxc3ep
3. Kxc3

☐ *Pawn endings / Defending (rook pawn): B*
1) 1. f4 (1. Ke4 Kg4!; 1. ... Kg5? 2. Kxe5 h4 3. f4+ Kh6 4. Ke4!) 1. ... exf4+ 2.
Kxf4
2) 1. g5 Kg4 2. Kxc4 Kxg5 3. Kd3 Kg4 4. Ke2 Kg3 5. Kf1
3) 1. Ka1! Kc1 2. Ka2 Kc2 3. Ka1 Kb3 4. a4!
4) 1. a4 Kb4 2. a5 Kxa5 3. Ka3
5) 1. Kb6 (1. a6? bxa6 2. Kxc6 Kb4) 1. ... c5 2. a6! bxa6 3. Kxc5
6) 1. ... Kd4 (1. ... h4 2. Kf5 h3 3. gxh3 Kd6 4. Kf6 Kd7 5. h4 Ke8 6. Kg7; 1.
... Kc6 2. Kf5) 2. Kf5 Ke3 3. Kg5 Kf2
7) 1. ... Kd2 (1. ... Kc2 2. Ke6 Kd3 3. Kd5) 2. Ke6 Ke3 3. Kd5 Kf4
8) 1. ... Kh1
9) 1. ... Kf1 (1. ... Kh1 2. Kf2 Kh2 3. Ke3 Kg3 4. Kd4 Kf4 5. Kc5 Ke5 6. Kb6
Kd6 7. Kxa6) 2. Kf3 Ke1 3. Ke3 Kd1 4. Kd3 Kc1 5. Kc4 Kb2 6. Kc5 Kb3
7. Kb6
10) 1. Kd7 (1. Kd6 h5) 1. ... h5 2. Ke8 Kg5 3. Kf7
11) 1. a3 Kb3 2. a4 Kxa4 3. Kxc2 Ka3 4. Kb1
12) 1. ... Kh3 ½-½

171

9⁺   The discovered attack

AIM OF THE LESSON
- learning to set up a battery

PRIOR KNOWLEDGE
- The discovered attack
- The preparatory move 'targeting'

ACQUISITION

Instruction
With a discovered attack we are making use of a battery – no battery, no discovered attack. If there is not yet a battery, then we can set one up by correctly positioning the back piece or the front piece.

Setting up the back piece
This diagram (⇨) illustrates a simple example. White plays **1. Qg7+**. The queen turns into the back piece and forces the target piece on to a fateful square. After **1. ... Kb1**, first **2. Bg6+** and then **3. Qxa7** decide matters. It is important that the queen on a7 is controlling the g1-square.
Positions like this, in which we can position the back piece with tempo (with a check), are simple. What is slightly harder is setting up a battery with a quiet move. In this diagram (⇩) White's material advantage is far from being enough for a win. White will have to capture the black rook. His first move is a powerful one: **1. Ra5**. The black king cannot escape the discovered check. What is noticeable is that the black rook does not have much space for manoeuvre either. Only a check is possible: **1. ... Re4+** (1. ... Rb4 2. Nd3+ or 1. ... Rd8 2.

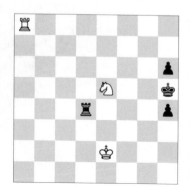

172

Nf7+), but after **2. Kf3** (2. Kd3? Rf4!) Black loses his rook to a discovered check.

In the next two examples the battery is not easy to spot at first glance. In this diagram (⇧) Black has just taken a pawn by Rxe4. After all, the d-pawn is pinned. White must now find a clever way to move his queen out of danger. Black was no doubt hoping for 1. Qg5 (with the threats of 2. Qxd8+ and 2. cxd3), but 1. ... Rxd3 (1. ... Re1+ is also possible) 2. Rxd3 Re1# refutes the queen move. On the other hand **1. Qg2** is strong. Now the threat is simply **2. dxe4**, but that is more than enough. The black rook cannot move away because of **2. Rf8+** winning the queen.

The position in the diagram (⇨) comes from the game Shirov–Korchnoi, Plovdiv 2003. White has just played the mysterious move Kh2. It is actually a primitive trap. Black fell into it with **1. ... Nxf2 2. Bxf2 Re2**. It appears that the double attack with the rook is enough to win back the piece. Unfortunately for Korchnoi. White can play **3. Ra2**; the bishop on c2 is now protected and so is the bishop on f2 indirectly. **3. ... Rxf2** would be followed by **4. Bxh7+**.

Setting up the front piece
In the diagram (⇩) White is fighting against two far advanced passed pawns. It seems that there is no way to parry the threat of 1. ... g2. The subject of this lesson must come to his aid: **1. Be1**. White sets up the front piece, and it is all sorted. Black cannot get a queen (**1. ... f1Q 2. Bc3+**) and he can no longer play **1. ... g2** on account of **2. Bxf2**. The move **1. ... Kg6** is followed by **2. Bxf2 gxf2 3. Kxc5**, and after **1. ... c4** Black has no prospects after **2. Bxf2 gxf2 3. Rf1**.

In the upper part of the diagram (⇧) a front piece is set up, but eliminating a defender also plays a role. White plays **1. Nf7**. The rook on h8 which is under attack cannot move because of 2. Nd6+. The best is **1. ... Rxf7**.

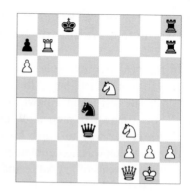

The winning discovered attack in the lower part) is more frequent in practice. Black plays **1. ... Ne2+ 2. Kh1 Ng3+**.

At first glance the position in the diagram (⇨) appears to have nothing to do with the subject. Have the students first of all analyse it on their own.

White has a few nice tries with 1. Rf5 or 1. Rh5, but in both cases Black holds the draw with 1. ... Rd4. Whether the king can get involved or not plays a decisive part. Without the king the white b-pawn can never reach the opposing back rank. So White must start with **1. Kd6**. Thanks to the battery, Black cannot for the moment follow the white king: 1. ... Kd8? 2. Kc5+. The rest is a matter of technique (see next lesson). Black can no longer put up any resistance, e.g. **1. ... Rb2 2. Kc7 Rc2+ 3. Kb7 Rh2 4. b6 Ke7 5. Ra5!** The b-pawn costs Black a rook. The h-pawn cannot do any damage since the black king cannot make it across the 5th rank.

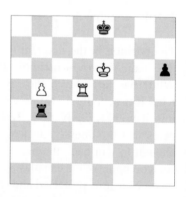

Setting up the front and target pieces
Nothing is as yet visible: neither a battery nor any loot. It is remarkable how simply many things can be made possible. In the upper half of the diagram (⇩) White wins with **1. Bb7 Rb8** (1. ... a6 2. Re5+). The battery is ready and the target piece is there: **2. Bc6+**.

In the bottom half **1. ... Nf1+ 2. Kg1 Nd2+** is the winning continuation.

174

White's material advantage in this diagram (♙) is normally not enough to be able to win. However, White can win the bishop (and then there is a win, though a difficult one!). After **1. Nd5** Black has a choice, but no matter where the bishop goes, it is lost: **1. ... Bg1 2. Nc3+ Kb2 3. Ne2+**. Ask the students to refute the other bishop moves. On the third move White can always choose his discovered check in such a way that the bishop is lost.

In lesson 14 we saw an example of a battery which kept on being reloaded. We find a similar example in this diagram (♟), only there is as yet no battery. White prepares things with **1. Bg8+ Kh8**. The battery is there now and the rest speaks for itself: **2. Bxe6+ Kh7 3. Bg8+ Kh8 4. Bxd5+ Kh7 5. Bg8+ Kh8 6. Bxc4+ Kh7 7. Bg8+ Kh8 8. Bxb3+ Kh7 9. Bg8+ Kh8 10. Bxa2+ Kh7 11. Bg8+!** (the battery needs to be reloaded again, since 11. Bxb1 Bxb1 is not enough for a win) **11. ... Kh8 12. Bb3+ Kh7 13. Bxc2+ Qxc2+ 14. Rxc2**.

PRACTICE

Reminder
◊ *Setting up a battery*

Workbook

☐ *Discovered attack / Setting up a battery: A*
Explanation: In the starting position there is not yet a battery. A winning battery can be set up with tempo.
Mistake: The task is too difficult.
Help: Look for an unprotected piece belonging to your opponent. Attack it in such a way that you set up a battery at the same time.

☐ *Discovered attack / Setting up a battery: B*
Explanation: See exercise page A.

ANSWERS

☐ *Discovered attack / Setting up a battery: A*
1) 1. Qe2 Qe7 2. Qxa6 Kd8 3. 0-0
2) 1. Qg4 g6 2. Nh6+
3) 1. Qf3 0-0 2. Nf6+
4) 1. Qa4+ Bd7 (1. ... Qd7 2. Bb5 ; 1. ... Kd8 2. Rd1) 2. Bf7+
5) 1. Qd5 Qc1+ 2. Rf1+
6) 1. Rd1+ Kg7 2. Bh6+
7) 1. ... Rg8 2. Qxe1 Bxd4+ 3. Kh1 Rg1#
8) 1. ... Qb6 2. Qf2 (2. Rac7 Rxg4+ 3. Kf2 (3. Kh1 Qxe3 4. fxg4 Be4#) 3. ... Rg2+ 4. Kxg2 Qxe3) 2. ... Qxa7
9) 1. Qb4 Na6 2. Nxc8++ Ke8 3. Qe7#
10) 1. ... Qf7 2. Re7 Rg1+ 3. Rxg1 Qxh5
11) 1. ... Qg5+ 2. Kh2 Qh6+
12) 1. Qc5 (1. Qe7+ Kg8 2. Rd8+ Kh7 3. Rxc8 Rxc8) 1. ... Qxc5 (1. ... Qb8 2. Rd8#) 2. Rd8#

☐ *Discovered attack / Setting up a battery: B*
1) 1. Bb3 Ke5 (1. ... Qg7+ 2. Rg4+) 2. Rc5+
2) 1. Qd8 (1. Qc8 Ke7) 1. ... Qb1+ 2. Bg6#
3) 1. Bd3 Qg1 2. Kc3#
4) 1. Rh4! (1. Rg6+? Kf7 2. Bh5 Rd5 3. Rg5+ (3. Kh4 Be4! 4. Rg4+ Rxh5+ 5. Kxh5 Bf3) 3. ... Kf6) 1. ... Bd5 (1. ... Be4 2. Bf3) 2. Be6+
5) 1. Bh3 Rxc7 (1. ... Kxc7 2. Rc4+ Kd8 3. Rc8#) 2. Rg8#
6) Drawing (Dutch national women's champion Peng – 13x!)
7) 1. Qb1+ Kg2 2. Rxf2+
8) 1. Rf8 Rxh7 2. Kg6+
9) 1. Qb3 Kf5 (1. ... Bc5 2. Ng5+ ; 1. ... Qh7 2. Ng5+; 1. ... g5 2. Qe6+ Kf3 3. Ne5+) 2. Nh6+ gxh6 3. Qxg8
10) 1. Bf1 g1Q 2. Bd3+
11) 1. Qc8 Kf7 (1. ... Bf5 2. Qxf5) 2. Bc5
12) 1. Qb5 Ke4 (1. ... Qa1 2. Bd4+ Kxd4 3. Qe5+; 1. ... Qc1 2. Bxa3+; 1. ... Qd1 2. Qd7+; 1. ... Qe4 2. Qb7+; 1. ... Qe6 2. Qb3+; 1. ... Qh4 2. Be7+; 1. ... Qg3 2. Bf2+; 1. ... Qh1 2. Qb7+; 1. ... Ke6 2. Qe8+; 1. ... Bxf4 2. Bf2+) 2. Qe8+

10⁺ Endgame technique

AIM OF THE LESSON
• improving endgame abilities

PRIOR KNOWLEDGE
• all endgame topics so far

ACQUISITION

Instruction
The ideal: winning won positions and drawing in bad positions. Who does not want to be able to do that? In this lesson we give some guidelines which Step 4 players can bear in mind and which they can also make use of in their own games.

One important question which has to be asked in every position: What do I know about this position? Let us take as an example the following diagram (⇨). It is clear that White can only win if he gives up his rook for the bishop + pawn. Knowledge about key squares (previous Step) is required here, It is not enough to play 1. Rxe5 dxe5 2. Kd6 Kf7 3. Kxe5 Ke7 with a draw. However, giving check first does win: **1. Rf5+ Ke8** (1. ... Ke7 2. Rxe5+ dxe5 3. Kxe5 Kd7 4. Kf6) **2. Ke6 Kd8** (2. ... Bg3 3. Rg5) **3. Rf7**, followed by **4. Rd7** and **5. Rxd6**. If Black takes the rook then the white king is directly on a key square.
1. Rh7+ Ke8 2. Ke6 Kd8 3. Rd7+ is also a possibility.
You also need to mate your opponent. So you can hardly do without pawns. In this diagram (⇩) White has only one pawn left. Cutting off the opposing king with 1. Bh2 looks very

tempting, but unfortunately after 1. .. b3 2. Kc3 b2 3. Kxb2 g1Q 4. Bxg1 Kd6 the final pawn is gone. White must start with **1. Kc4** and only after **1. ... Kd6** play **2. Bh2+**.

In general, when you have an advantage in material you should swap off pieces, but not too many pawns.

Another good piece of advice is not to under-estimate your opponent's possibilities. The game is not over till your opponent has resigned or been mated. In this diagram (⇨) 1. b7 looks obvious. After 1. ... Rb8 (1. ... f6+ 2. Kd4 Rb8 3. Kc5) 2. g4 f6+ 3. Kd4 Kd6 4. Rb6+ Kc7 5. Kc5 Black cannot go in for an endgame. Have the students work this out for themselves. This is all very instructive, but there is a cold shower awaiting White if Black meets 1. b7 with 1. ... Rc4. Mate with 2. ... f6# can no longer be prevented. White can make a good start with **1. g4**. After, for example, **1. ... f6+ 2. Kd4 Kd6 3. b7 e5+ 4. Ke4 Rb8 5. h4** he is despite everything in the driving seat.

In this diagram (⇩) it is Black to move. Have the students make some suggestions. The prudent 1. ... Ree8 (2. Rc8 is seen as a threat to be taken seriously) leads to a disadvantage after 2. Rf5 b4 3. Rb5 Rb8 4. Rc7. An even worse move is 1. ... b4 (a popular suggestion) 2. Rc8 Rb5 3. Rfd1 Rxb7 4. R1d8. The game continued 1. ... Rb8? 2. Rc8+ Re8 3. Rxe8+ Rxe8 4. Rc1 resigned. The correct move is **1. ... Re7**, and Black wins the b-pawn (**2. Rc8 Rxb7**).

In this lesson we first of all follow the order of the advice given in the reminder in the workbook. "Think first, then move" is an important basic principle. Students tend to look no further once they have discovered an apparently good move. Neither at whether the move is really as good as it looks, nor for better moves. In this diagram (⇧) 1. Bd2 is a move which wins a pawn, but not the game. Black defends with the cunning 1. ... Bg7 2. Bxf4 (2. Kxf4? Bh6+) 2. ... Bh8, and it soon becomes clear that White is not going to make any further progress. Black moves his bishop back and forward between h8 and g7. The correct way is **1. Bd8+ Bg5 2. Bf6!** (easily overlooked). If White captured on g5 Black would win; now he loses on the spot.

The position in the diagram (⇨) is best played to a finish as a simultaneous, or else by the students between one another. The trainer takes the black pieces. After the game is finished, discussing it as a group is recommended. White has an (unimportant) pawn more, but Black has an active rook. With correct play the chances will be about equal, but if White does not choose the correct continuation, Black can rapidly have a very good position. Some possibilities are:

1. h3
Safety first. The rook on e1 cannot take any part in the game till the back rank mate has been prevented. Now there is also the threat of 2. Re7, and so Black has no time for 1. ... Rb2. After 1. Nd4 Rb2 2. a3 Kf8 3. Ra1 Bb5 4. a4 (or 4. Nxb5 Rxb5 5. c4 Rb2 6. Rc1 Ra2 with active play) 4. ... Bc4 Black is better.
1. ... Kf8 2. Re4!
The only way for the rook to become active.
2. ... Rb2
Other options are: 2. ... c5 3. dxc6ep Bxc6 4. Rb4 Rc8 5. Nd4, and White is better, or 2. ... Rb1+ 3. Kh2 Rb2 4. Rc4 Rxa2 5. Rxc7 Ke8 6. Nd4 as in the main variation. **3. Rc4 Rxa2 4. Rxc7 Ke8 5. Nd4**
The chances are roughly level.

When discussing it afterwards, it is above all the games which were played which should be dealt with.

It is good fun to deal with the examples which have been given as a group, but it is better to select examples from games played by the students. Well known material is gone over again and along the way new knowledge, abilities or rules crop up. Their own games motivate the students better than 'strange' (to them) examples.

Let us take a look at an extract from the game Louisa Hohmann - Maria Hort, played in a German Girls championship under 12 year. According to the situation a greater or lesser number of the rules and variations which have been indicated should be dealt with. In this diagram (⇨) it is Black to move.

1. ... Bc1+ 2. Kb1 Bf4+

An amusing moment. Black has discovered that the bishop on g3 is unprotected and stops thinking. Of course 2. ... Ba3+ 3. Be1 Rxe1# is not difficult, but the variation does have to be discovered.

3. Kb2 Bxg3 4. Rc8+

Neither player notices that the opposing kings do not have a lot of space available. Even in the endgame you can play attacking chess. One strong move is 4. Nd7 Bd6 (4. ... Rf8 5. Nxf8 Kxf8 6. Rc5 is pretty hopeless) 5. Rc8+ Bf8 (see the diagram ⇩).

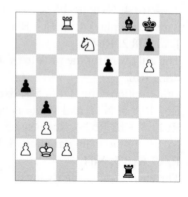

Black is in trouble; only the rook and the e-pawn can still move. White has various ways to win. In such cases you should always go for the safest way, in which you almost do not have to think about things: 6. c4 (the white king has to join in) 6. ... bxc3+ 7. Kc2 (careful: 7. Kxc3? Rc1+) 7. ... e5 8. a3 e4 9. Nxf8 Rxf8 10. Rxf8+ Kxf8 11. Kxc3 with a simple win.

4. ... Rf8 5. Rc5 Rf5 6. Rc8+ Rf8 7. Rxf8+ Kxf8 (see the diagram ⇧) **8. Nc4**

Always try to kill two birds with one stone. From c6 the knight stops the a-pawn and at the same time keeps the opposing king at a distance: 8. Nc6 Bc7 9. c3 bxc3+ 10. Kxc3 Ke8 11. Kc4 Kd7 12. Kb5 with chances for White.

8. ... Bc7 9. c3 bxc3+ 10. Kxc3 Ke7 11. Kd4

In the meantime Black is better. Here and in the subsequent course of the game White should be following the rule: 'Exchange as many pawns as possible': 11. b4 axb4+ 12. Kxb4 Kf6 13. Kb5 Kxg6 14. a4 Kf5 15. a5 Bxa5 16. Kxa5 g5 17. Kb4 g4 18. Kc3 g3 19. Kd3 Kf4 20. Ke2 with a draw.

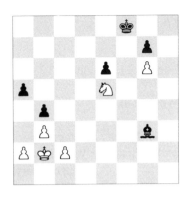

11. ... Kf6 12. Ke4

Active play would be: 12. Kc5!

12. ... Kxg6 13. Kf3

Exchanging pawns with 13. a3 is still possible.

13. ... e5 14. Ne3 Kh5 15. Kg3 g5 16. Kh3 e4 17. a3 Bb6 18. Ng2 (see diagram ⇨)

For the moment White's position is not all that great, but after 18. Nf1 the knight would again have more squares.

18. ... e3

Limit your opponent's options: 18. ... Bf2! 19. b4 axb4 20. axb4 e3, and Black wins.

19. Kg3 g4 20. Nf4+ Kg5 21. Ne2 Bc7+ 22. Kg2 Kh4 23. a4 Kg5 24. Nd4 Be5 25. Ne2 (see diagram ⇩)

Here the game was agreed a draw, but Black could have secured the full point quite simply with 25. ... Kf5 26. Kf1 Ke4 27. Nc1 g3 28. Kg2 Bc7.

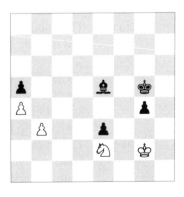

Not all moves which might be possible need to be mentioned. What is important above all is to bring out the general rules.

Reminder
Endgame technique

Workbook

☐ *Endgame / Strategy: A*
  Explanation: Which plan should be followed by the side which has the move?
             That can vary from activating a piece to restricting the opponent's
             options.
  Mistake: The wrong plan is chosen.
  Help: Play out the position on a board.
  Mistake: The student does not understand the task.
  Help: Ask targeted questions. Which piece is not well played? What
             move does the opponent want to make?

☐ *Endgame / Strategy: B*
  Explanation: See exercise page A.

☐ *Endgame / Tactics: A*
☐ *Endgame / Tactics: B*
  Explanation: The side whose move it is can win material (sometimes only a
             pawn) or deliver mate.

☐ *Rook ending / Strategy: A*
  Explanation: Activate the king or place it on the correct square. In some po-
             sitions the passed pawn has to be promoted. These are some of
             the options open to the students in these tasks.

☐ *Rook ending / Vulnerability: A*
  Explanation: The opponent's king and/or rook are so unfortunately placed,
             that the side whose move it is can take advantage of this fact.

☐ *Endgame / Vulnerability: A*
  Explanation: The side with the rook can win the opponent's bishop. Well-
             known combinatory motifs such as the double attack and the
             pin can help here.
  Mistake: The student cannot manage the task.
  Help: Point out which type of combination is the winning one (e.g.
             double attack, X-ray check or pin).

☐ *Endgame / Strategy: A*
1) 1. c5 bxc5 2. Nc4
2) 1. Rc1 (1. Kf2 Bc2 2. Rc1 Bd3 3. Rc5 Bc4 4. a3 Kd8; 1. Re2 b4; in both cases White doesn't make easy progress) 1. ... Kd8 2. Kf2 Kd7 3. Ke3
3) 1. ... e4 2. Rd1 Rf8
4) 1. b5 (otherwise Black plays b5); 1. a4 is also possible.
5) 1. ... a4 2. Kc2 axb3+ 3. Kxb3 Ng6 and Nh4
6) 1. b4 The bishop on a3 is lost! The white king goes to b3.
7) 1. g5 (exchanges the black passed pawn for a less important pawn) 1. ... Bxg5 (1. ... Be5 2. f4) 2. Rxc3
8) 1. d5 (otherwise Black blocks the d-pawn with Nd5; White remains with a bad bishop) 1. ... Ne8 1. ... Nxd5 2. Bxg7 and White is slightly better.
9) 1. b4 axb4+ 2. cxb4
10) 1. a5 (otherwise Black keeps his pawn structure together with Kc6)
11) 1. ... d4+ 2. Kxd4 Nd5 3. g3 Nxb4
12) 1. ... Be5 2. Rxc6 bxc6

☐ *Endgame / Strategy: B*
1) 1. Ra2 (1. Rf2 Ra7) 1. ... Rb7 2. Ra6
2) 1. ... a5 (prevents White from creating a passed pawn on the c-file with b4)
3) 1. ... c6 2. Ne6 cxb5 3. axb5 a4
4) Drawing (Genna Sosonko)
5) 1. Ke2 (the king must be activated in the ending)
6) 1. Ng1 (knight to a better square)
7) 1. ... f6 (1. ... c5 2. Bxe5+ Bxe5 3. Rd1)
8) 1. Qd6+ Qxd6 (1. ... Kg8 2. Qxb6 axb6 3. Nd6) 2. Nxd6
9) 1. Bf7 Kb4 2. Bg6 Ka3 3. Kf1 Ng3+ 4. Kf2
10) 1. ... Ne5 2. Qb8+ Kh7 3. Qxb5 Ng4+ 4. Kg1 Qb3
11) 1. Rd7 Re8 2. Rc4
12) 1. Bg5 (1. Ng5 Bxg5 2. Bxg5 and because of the opposite coloured bishops the win is difficult)

☐ *Endgame / Tactics: A*
1) 1. Nd4 Kg3 (1. ... Qd8 2. Ne6+) 2. Nc6
2) 1. d4+ Kxd4 2. Rc8
3) 1. ... b5 (1. ... Ra1+ 2. Kh2 b5 Nd2) 2. Nd6 (2. Rd7 Ra1+ 3. Kh2 Bg1+) 2. ... Be5 3. Nxb5 Ra1+
4) 1. Nc7 Bd4 2. Ne6+
5) 1. ... Ra5

6) 1. Ne3! Rd4 (1. ... Ra4 2. Nd5 Kd7 3. Rxe7+ Kd6 4. Rd7+) 2. Rxe7+
7) 1. Rh6 g4 2. hxg4+
8) 1. ... Raf8 (2. Rhf1 Bxe4)
9) 1. Rdc3 Rc8 2. Rxb6
10) 1. Ka1 (1. Nd2 Ne3 2. Ka1 Nc2+ 3. Kb1) 1. ... Ne3 (1. ... Be3 2. Ne1 Bc1
    3. Nc2# ; 1. ... Be1 2. Nxe1 Ne3 3. Kb1 Nd5 4. Nc2#) 2. Nd4 Be1 3. Nb5#
11) 1. Rcb1 Rd7 2. c6
12) 1. ... Ra8 2. Bc1 Ra1

☐ *Endgame / Tactics: B*
 1) 1. ... b5 2. Bxb5 Ncd4+
 2) 1. Nb7+ Ka6 2. Nc5+
 3) 1. Rf1 Qxf1 2. Ng3+
 4) 1. Qc1+ Kb3 2. Qb2+ Kc4 3. Qb4#
 5) 1. h6 Bf8 2. Bd5
 6) 1. Bh5 Bxh5 2. Rxh6
 7) 1. Rc8+ Qxc8 2. bxc8Q+ Rxc8 3. Rb7#
 8) 1. ... h5 2. axb6 Bd3#
 9) 1. Qg7+ Kc4 (1. ... Kd3 2. Be4+; 1. ... Ke3 2. Qg1+; 1. ... Kc5 2. Qg1+) 2.
    Bd5+
10) 1. Bh3 Bh4 2. Re1+
11) 1. h8Q+ Kxh8 2. Kg6
12) 1. Rd1+ Kc8 2. Ra1

☐ *Rook ending / Strategy: A*
 1) 1. Kf3 Rd7 2. Ke3 Rc7 3. Rc2 Kg7 4. d4 with advantage (activating the
    king).
 2) 1. Rd1 (1. h3 Rc1+ 2. Kh2 Ra1 3. Rd5 is less good. The rook belongs
    behind the passed pawn)
 3) 1. ... Rd8 (1. ... Rc8 2. a4) 2. Re3 Rd4
 4) 1. h6 Kxh6 (1. ... a4 2. hxg7 a3 3. g8Q+ Kxg8 4. Rc8+) 2. Rc8
 5) 1. ... Kd6 2. Rxb5 Ra8
 6) 1. Re7 (1. Kg6 Kf8 2. Rh1 Ke7=) 1. ... Kf8 2. Rb7
 7) 1. Ra8 Kc2 2. Rc8+
 8) 1. Kg4 (1. Rxg7 Kf3) 1. ... a6 2. Rxg7
 9) 1. e4 dxe4 2. Ke8 Rh8+ 3. f8Q Rxf8+ 4. Kxf8 Kb6 5. Rxh2 Kc5 6. Rh4
10) 1. Re2 (1. Rxe3 Rxb2) 1. ... Rd3 2. Rxe3
11) 1. ... b4 2. Kf2 a4
12) 1. b4!

□ *Rook ending / Vulnerability: A*
1) 1. c3 Rg4 2. Ra8#
2) 1. Kg7 Rf8 2. Re5+ Kd7 3. Kxf8+
3) 1. Rg7 Rxh6 (1. ... Rxg7 2. hxg7 Kxb3 3. g8Q+ Kxb2 4. Qc4) 2. Rxb7+
4) 1. Kb7 Ra5 (1. ... Rc8 2. Rd1+) 2. b4 axb3 3. Rxa5
5) 1. Kf6 Kxf3 (1. ... c1Q 2. Rf5#; 1. ... Rxf3 2. Rh4#) 2. Rh3+
6) 1. Rh1 Rd8 (1. ... Kf4 2. Rh4+ Kg3 3. Rxd4 Kf2 4. Ke5 Kxe2 5. Ke4 Kf2
   6. Kd3 e2 7. Rf4+) 2. Rh4#
7) 1. ... e1Q 2. Rxe1 Kf2
8) 1. Ra5 (1. Ra1 d4 2. Re1+ Kd5) 1. ... Rd8!? 2. Kxd8 Kxf5 3. Rxd5+ Ke4 4.
   Rd1 f5 5. Re1+
9) 1. Kf7 Re1 2. Rh8#
10) 1. Rd3+ (1. c8N Rxh3=) 1. ... Kxd3 2. c8Q
11) 1. Re7 (1. Rf7+ Ke6 2. Rf6+ Ke7 3. Rxg6 is better for White) 1. ... Ra3+ 2.
    Re3 Rxa7 3. Re5#
12) 1. Ke1 Rh2 2. Ra2+ Kb4 3. c3+

□ *Endgame / Vulnerability: A*
1) 1. Rg1+ Kd2 2. Kb3
2) 1. Rb7 Bd4 2. Re7+
3) 1. Rf5+ Kg1 2. Re5 Bb5 3. Re1+ Bf1 4. Ra1
4) 1. Kc7 Ba6 (1. ... Bd7 2. Rh6+) 2. Rh6+
5) 1. Rf3 Bg4 (1. ... Bg2 2. Rg3+ ; 1. ... Bc8 2. Rf8+) 2. Rg3
6) 1. Ke4 Bh2 2. Rg2 Be5 3. Rg6+
7) 1. Rf5 Bg4 2. Rf4+
8) 1. Kf3 Bc7 2. Re8+ Kg7 3. Re7+
9) Drawing (Kasparov)
10) 1. Ke3 Bh1 2. Rg1 Be4 3. Rg5+
11) 1. Rb8 Ke7 2. Ra8! Ke8 3. Kd6
12) 1. Kf6 Bb3 (1. ... Ba2 2. Ra5+ ; 1. ... Be8 2. Rc8+) 2. Ra5+ Kb7 3. Rb5+

11⁺   Chess problems

AIM OF THE LESSON
- to increase reasoning ability

PRIOR KNOWLEDGE
- solving strategies

ACQUISITION

Instruction
As well as normal competitive chess, the world
of chess also has other disciplines: correspond-
ence chess and chess composition (sub-divid-
ed into endgame studies and chess problems).
Chess problems are the most different from
normal chess, which in itself is reason enough
for many trainers to omit this chapter. They are
unknown and therefore unloved!

Chess problems have nothing to do with chess
games, all they have in common are the rules of
play! We shall explain any special rules with the
help of this diagram (⇩). A problem sets a very
specific task, in this case mate in four moves. In
the sort of problems we will be taking a look at
it is always White to move. The solution does
not appear to be much of a problem, since 1.
e8Q d1Q 2. Qh8+ Qh5 3. Qxh5# is even mate
in three. How can Black delay the mate? That is
possible with 1. ... d1N+ 2. Kg3 Ne3! In order
to stick with the task as it was set, there must
now be a mate in two, but that is not possible:
3. Qe4+ (3. Qxe3 is stalemate) 3. ... Kg1, and
the g2-square is not available.

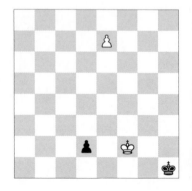

Mate in four is however possible with **1. e8R
d1N+** (1. ... d1Q 2. Rh8+) **2. Kg3 Ne3 3. Rxe3
Kg1 4. Re1#.**

Apparent from being 'neat', is this also instructive? Yes, solving problems certainly makes sense (quite apart from the fact that one is also quite at liberty to do something from time to time which is not only useful but also pleasurable!), because:
• it encourages logical thinking
• it is good for creativity
In addition to that, all sorts of abilities are required which come from practical play. Taking into account the strongest defence is one of these abilities (the key to the first problem). In addition it is a simple way to learn how to make use of zugzwang.

In the diagram (⇧) the task is: White is to mate in two moves. The immediate 1. Bf7 is stalemate. The correct way to think in such positions is: What will Black do on his next move? Mate in two will follow after 1. ... Bf7 2. Bxf7# and 1. ... Bd5 2. Bf7# (it prevents interposing on g8). So the best defence is 1. ... Be6, in order to interpose with the bishop on c8 or g8. White must make a move after which the Bc8 can no longer spoil things for him. So the correct waiting move is **1. Rd8!**

In the diagram (⇨) we can follow a similar process. What is Black going to play? Simply 1. ... Nf7 prevents mate on the second move (1. ... Ng8 2. Rh7# or 1. ... Ng4 2. Ra8#). From f7 the knight can either capture on d8 and be used to interpose on e8. White can avoid all this with **1. Re7!**

In the diagram (⇩) we think things out logically. We start with some analysis. Black has two legal moves: 1. ... cxb5 and 1. ... Ka4. Which mating patterns are hiding in this position? White can play 1. c4, so that after 1. ... cxb5 he has 2. Qxb5# up his sleeve. But where is the mate after 1. ... Ka4? To prevent the king

move White can start with **1. c3 Ka4 2. Qb4#**.
After **1. c3 cxb5**, too. White has a chance to
mate: **2. Qa7#**.

The aim of the tasks is known: mate (in
two). So we can invest all our energy in the
analysis of the problem and in the weighing
up of various solutions with the help of the
information supplied by the analysis.

In the diagram (⇧) we quickly establish that
White must promote the pawn, or else no
mating pattern is possible. After the promotion
the king cannot go to the 7th rank. The only
squares still accessible to it are d6 and f6,
according to which piece White chooses. We
can now continue to think the way we did in
the other examples. We choose a different
solving strategy. We go through the limited
number of solutions in order and eliminate the
moves which do not lead to mate.

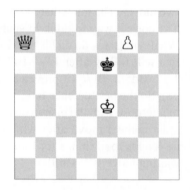

A) 1. f8Q fails on account of stalemate.
B) 1. f8R Kd6 and mate in one is not possible.
C) **1. f8B Kf6 2. Qf5#**. That's it!
We can stop here and execute the move.
This method by elimination is also a helpful
one in many positions in practical play. Moves
A, B and D lose. That only leaves move C
after which I cannot see a direct win for my
opponent. Here we go, I'll make the move –
now it is up to my opponent to find the correct
continuation.

In this diagram (⇨) we follow the same proce-
dure. Promotion to a rook is required: **1. f8R
Kd6 2. Rf6#**.

We move the kings two files to the left, and
the result is the diagram (⇩). Once more we
go through the various options in order. We
cunningly pass by the promotion to a rook and
a bishop: we have already seen that. Now it is
the knight's turn: **1. f8N Kd6 2. Qc5#**. Not a
simple mating pattern.

For the sake of completeness, we also take a look at the fourth possible promotion. The German composer Speckmann is the one responsible for this amusing quartet. This diagram too (⇧) is remarkably like the previous one. However, the only way for White to manage to mate in two is by promoting to a queen. This is logical, because the black king can get away to b5, which in itself is not very far but which offers the king other escape squares. **1. f8Q Kb5** is followed by **2. Qfc5#**. Have the students solve this task in their heads.

Let us raise the level of difficulty of the positions a little. In this diagram (⇨) some mating patterns can be sound (queen on a4 and b2), but moves like 1. Qe2 or 1. Qe8 fail to 1. ... Kb4. As soon as the black king is on b4, it becomes impossible to construct any mating pattern. Conclusion: White must prevent Kb4. After **1. Qe1** there may be no threat of mate, but since Black cannot skip a move he must make his own position worse. Black is in zugzwang, every pawn move leads to mate: **1. ... d3 2. Qc3#**; **1. ... c4 2. Qe7#** and **1. ... b5 2. Qa5#**. Without the correct analysis (the king must not be allowed to move to b4) it is almost impossible to solve this problem. But if you go about it the correct way it becomes do-able.

In this diagram (⇩) Black is almost in zugzwang. After a bishop or a pawn move White can deliver mate (**2. Qa4#** or **2. Qf8#**). Nor is **1. ... Ka3** a problem: **2. Qxa5#**. It is only after 1. ... Kc4 that a mate is not yet possible. The solution must fulfil two conditions:
• White must be able to deliver mate after Kc4.
• The queen must control f8, a4 and a5.
• Conclusion of the analysis: the queen cannot move, the king must keep control of the b3-square, so the solution must be

a bishop move. On e8 the bishop gets in the way of the queen move to f8; all that is left is **1. Bd7**. It is mate after **1. ... Kc4 2. Qe4#**.

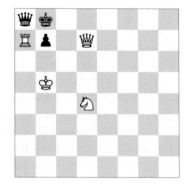

In the following diagram (⇑) we find a final example with zugzwang. Once again, we remind you how important it is to ask what the opponent's next move will be. In endgames in which the opponent does not have many moves, zugzwang often has a role to play. Every move by Black leads to mate: 1. ... Qxa7 2. Qd8#; 1. ... Kxa7 2. Nc6#; 1. ... b6 2. Qc7#. White must make a waiting move which retains all the possibilities for mate. So the king, rook and knight cannot move. The queen must keep an eye on the c7- and d8-squares, which can be done properly from e7. The extra option which Black then gets (the king gets the use of the c8-square) in no way prevents a mate: **1. Qe7 Kc8 2. Rxa8#**. After other moves by Black, White delivers mate as described above.

No matter how unnatural the solving of problems may appear (after all, there are umpteen other ways to win the game), let us nevertheless plead in favour of paying some attention to the type of problem illustrated in this lesson. Let us list another few useful things:
- take into account the strongest defence
- make use of zugzwang
- use the whole board
- visualise
- spot unknown mating patterns
- pieces must cooperate to as great an extent as possible
- solving problems encourages creativity

Reminder
◊ *Chess problems*

Workbook

☐ *Mate in two / Cooperation (♔♕): A*
Explanation: White to mate in two.
Mistake: The task is too difficult.
Help: Ask questions (according to the task) along the lines of: Which
             moves does the opposing king still have? Which mating patterns
             can you see? Can you give the opposing king an escape square?
             We must accept that some children just do not have an eye for
             problems.

☐ *Mate in two / Cooperation (♕♖): B*
☐ *Mate in two / Cooperation (♕♗): C*
☐ *Mate in two / Cooperation (♕♘): D*

☐ *Mate in two / Cooperation (♕♙): A*
1) 1. Qg7 d4 2. Qg2#
2) 1. Qe3 b1Q (1. ... b1N 2. Qb6#) 2. Qa3#
3) 1. Kd1 Kf1 2. Qe1#
4) 1. Qc8 Kh6 (1. ... h3 2. Qxh3#) 2. Qh8#
5) 1. d4 e4 (1. ... exd4 2. e4#) 2. Qc5#
6) 1. Qf6 Kg4 2. Qg5#
7) 1. Qe4 Kh5 2. Qh7#
8) 1. Qd4 Kxg5 (1. ... hxg5 2. Qh8# ; 1. ... c5 2. Qh4#) 2. Qe5#
9) 1. Qg7 Ka5 (1. ... Ka3 2. Qa1#) 2. Qa7#
10) 1. Kb7 Ka5 2. Qa6#
11) 1. Kf5 g5 (1. ... Kh6 2. Qh8#) 2. hxg6ep#
12) 1. Qa3 Kc4 (1. ... e3 2. Qb4#) 2. Qc5#

☐ *Mate in two / Cooperation (♕♖): B*
1) 1. Rb2 Ka6 (1. ... Ka4 2. Qa7#) 2. Qb6#
2) 1. Qb8 Kc4 2. Rc6#
3) 1. Kd3 Ke5 2. Qg5#
4) 1. Qb7 Kxh5 (1. ... Kf6 2. Rh6#) 2. Qh7#
5) 1. Rd2+ Kf3 2. Qd3#
6) 1. Ke4 Kd2 (1. ... Kf2 2. Qh2#) 2. Qb2#
7) 1. Qf7 Kc6 2. Ra6#
8) 1. Kd5 Kf4 (1. ... Kd3 2. Rg3#) 2. Qg3#

9) 1. Qh3 Kd2 (1. ... Kb2 2. Qb3#) 2. Qd3#

10) 1. Rd1 Ke2 (1. ... Kg2 2. Qd2#) 2. Qd2#

11) Drawing

12) 1. Qc2 Kh3 (1. ... Kf3 2. Rc3#) 2. Rc3#

☐ *Mate in two / Cooperation (♛♝): C*

1) 1. Qg2 Kh5 2. Qg5#

2) 1. Bf1 Kxf1 2. Qd1#

3) 1. Qf5 Kg3 2. Bf2#

4) 1. Qf4+ Kh5 2. Be8#

5) 1. Qc7 Kb4 (1. ... Ka6 2. Be2#) 2. Qc5#

6) 1. Qe7 Kb2 2. Qa3#

7) 1. Ba5 Kd7 2. Qe6#

8) 1. Qe8 Kf4 (1. ... Kh6 2. Qg6# ; 1. ... Kh4 2. Qh5#) 2. Qe3#

9) 1. Qf2 h5 (1. ... Kh5 2. Bf3# ; 1. ... Kh3 2. Be6#) 2. Be6#

10) 1. Bc2 exf6 (1. ... d6 2. Qf5# ; 1. ... Kxf6 2. Qf5# ; 1. ... d5 2. Qxe7#) 2. Bf5#

11) 1. Qe3 a4 (1. ... Ka4 2. Qb3# ; 1. ... c4 2. Qe8#) 2. Qxc5#

12) 1. Bf8 d4 (1. ... b5 2. Kd7#) 2. Ke6#

☐ *Mate in two / Cooperation (♛♞): D*

1) 1. Qf6 Kh5 (1. ... Kh3 2. Qh4#) 2. Qg5#

2) 1. Qh3+ Kg1 2. Nf3#

3) 1. Kb3 Kd1 (1. ... Kxb1 2. Qf1#) 2. Qf1#

4) 1. Ng2 Kf5 (1. ... Kh6 2. Qh4#) 2. Qf4#

5) 1. Qf1 Kg3 (1. ... Kh1 2. Nf3#) 2. Qh3#

6) 1. Qg8 Ke5 2. Qd5#

7) 1. Qa4 Kd3 2. Qc2#

8) 1. Nb7 Kd5 2. Qe4#

9) 1. Ne5+ Ke3 2. Qf2#

10) 1. Nd5 Ka6 (1. ... b6 2. Qxb6#) 2. Qb6#

11) 1. Ne6+ Kh5 (1. ... Kf5 2. Qf4#) 2. Qh2#

12) 1. Nd2 c4 2. Qd6#

List of concepts

alternative — A move which, besides the move played, comes into consideration.

blunder — A very bad move. The term is relative. At a lower level, a blunder allows mate or loss of a piece. At a higher level, a serious positional error is also considered to be a blunder.

centralising — Playing the pieces to the middle of the board so that they gain mobility.

centre — The middle of the chess board (the squares d4, d5, e4 and e5).

combination — A forced series of moves leading to mate, loss of material or a draw.

compensation — An advantage which compensates for a disadvantage. For instance, a large lead in development may compensate for the loss of a pawn.

connected — Two rooks of the same colour are connected if they are positioned on the same file or rank without any pieces intervening.

cutting off — A specific term for shielding off the king, usually with a rook or queen.

developing — Bringing out the pieces during the opening phase.

development — The extent to which one's pieces have been brought out.

duo — Two pawns of the same colour that are positioned next to each other on the same rank.

en prise — A French expression. A piece (other than the king) which is under attack is 'en prise'.

endgame — The final phase of a game, which arises after the middle game has ended. The separation between middlegame and endgame is to some extent arbitrary. An endgame typically arises after most of the pieces have been exchanged. Another characteristic of endgames is that the king can start to play an active role.

exchange — As a noun, it refers to the difference between a rook and a bishop or knight. The player who captures a protected rook with his bishop or knight wins the exchange, and so he has made a profitable exchange (or 'is the exchange up'). It makes a difference of two points.

flight square	A term that is mostly used to indicate a square to where the king may escape to. Less often used for other pieces.
forced move	The only move which does not straight-away lead to a loss. There is no reasonable alternative.
fork	A double attack with a knight (knight fork) or with a pawn (pawn fork).
gain of tempo	A move in which time is won because the opponent has to play a more or less forced move.
gambit	A sacrifice in the opening phase, usually in the form of a pawn.
getting a queen	A popular expression for pushing the pawn to the other side of the board. Strictly speaking, this is an inaccurate phrase because pieces other than the queen can be selected.
hanging	Insufficiently protected. A piece that is hanging (or 'dangling' - see also 'en prise') is being attacked, and the immediate threat is that it will be lost.
holding off	Making sure an enemy piece (mostly the king) can't reach a specific part of the board.
hole	A flight square for the castled king.
in-between-move	A (strong) move which precedes the 'logical' move (i.e. taking back or defending against an attack)
j'adoube	French for "I adjust", to be uttered immediately before readjusting a chess piece. This prevents a player from having to play with the piece touched.
kingside	The part of the board that consists of the e-, f-, g- and h-files.
line piece	Queen, rook or bishop.
line	A file, rank or diagonal.
major pieces	Queens and rooks.
middlegame	The phase of the game between the opening and the endgame.
minor pieces	Bishops and knights.
minor promotion	The promotion of a pawn to a rook, bishop or knight.
mobile pawn centre	Central pawns that have not been fixed.
opening	The initial phase of a game during which both sides develop their pieces.
passive	A term that refers to the position of a piece which lacks activity.
pawn structure	The way in which pawns of the same colour are grouped.
piece	Strictly speaking, this term refers to kings, queens, rooks, bishops and knights. In this manual, the expression 'pieces'

	is also used to refer to pieces and pawns collectively. Which of the two meanings is intended will be clear from the context.
place of battle	The part of the board where most of the action takes place.
ply	A term from computer chess which stands for half a move (i.e. a white or black move).
poisoned pawn	A pawn which a player is ill-advised to take.
queenside	The part of the board that consists of the a-, b-, c- and d-files.
quiet move	A (usually very strong) move that does not involve a check or a capture.
refute	Demonstrating that a certain move (or series of moves) is not correct.
resigning	Giving up a game before being mated. This only happens now and then at Step 4 level.
sacrifice	Giving up material voluntarily in order to gain another advantage or to avoid a greater disadvantage.
shielding off	Making sure the king can't reach a specific part of the board.
shouldering off	Making sure an enemy piece (mostly the king) can't reach a specific part of the board.
simultaneous display	A match in which one player plays against more than one player at the same time.
solving	To make a weakness disappear, e.g. undoubling a doubled pawn.
strategy	A long-term plan.
tactics	A move or series of moves to force a material gain, mate or a draw.
tempo	Indication for a move (Italian for 'time'). Plural: tempi.
temporary sacrifice	A sacrifice in which the sacrificed material is won back within the next couple of moves.
trap	A move which, while perhaps not objectively the best, entices the opponent to play an obvious but wrong move.
zugzwang	A situation in which the side that is to move cannot help but weaken his position.

The steps

Books

The following books are available in the 'Steps Method' series:

Manuals for chess trainers:	Step 1, Step 2, Step 3, Step 4, Step 5
Basic workbooks:	Stepping stones 1, Stepping stones 2, Step 1, Step 2, Step 3, Step 4, Step 5, Step 6
Extra workbooks:	Step 1 extra, Step 2 extra, Step 3 extra, Step 4 extra, Step 5 extra, Step 6 extra
Plus workbooks:	Step 1 plus, Step 2 plus, Step 3 plus, Step 4 plus, Step 5 plus
Manual for independent learners:	Step 6
Thinking ahead workbooks:	Step 2, *Stap 3*

The title represented in italic is only available in Dutch.

Updated information can be found at our website:
www.stappenmethode.nl (EN, FR, DE, NL)

All books can be ordered from this website for worldwide delivery:
www.stappenmethode.nl

Software

The Chess Tutor for Windows is a series of chess learning software based on the 'Steps Method'. **Chess Tutor Step 1**, **Chess Tutor Step 2** and **Chess Tutor Step 3** are available as download or as CD. You can first try the Chess Tutor using a free demo version.

More information at: http://www.chesstutor.eu/en